Inner Life Writes...

A Manifesto for RE-Connecting to Love, RE-Newing Your Mind & Radiating Your Light.

(Series Info: Part 2 of The Back to Love Series)

Denise James

Dedication

This book I dedicate to my mother.

Our mother-daughter road has been rocky at times, but you are an example of a true survivor, and I have ran with that baton and turned survivor into thriver.

Love you forever.

Acknowledgments

To Sean Patrick and Karen Mills-Alston at The Good House – thank you for your care and midwifery in supporting me with bringing this book to complete fruition and making the publication journey a smooth and seamless one.

Thanks to my King, Maurice Lennon, for being my ride and die and for giving me that space needed to make future calls for Dreams, and their realisation, possible.

Thanks to my family for being who you are and loving me as you do. You all know who you are. Acknowledgement to my parents who birthed me and in doing so, passed me the ancestral baton, to go and do better and move mountains. Especially thanks to my sons, Jermaine Moore and Jamal James, for being who you are and for the close bonds that we share that have never been broken and/or knocked adversely in anyway. It was a total pleasure raising you, my Kings. And thanks Jermaine, for all my grand babies and the experience of expanding my love through my experiences as Grandmother - there is no experience like it! Naz, Shakur, Megan, Ji and True, Nanny loves you!

Thank you to Pat, for unknowingly planting the idea that this book can be the accompanying Part Two to my first book **Back To Love**, so that people reading this Series may get a clearer picture of what life back to love looks and feels like, years on.

Thanks to every single client I have walked with in my work and role of Therapist. Every one of you are Bravehearts and blessings to planet earth for wanting to and carrying out your own independent investigation of "truth". In doing so, healing traumas and hurts whilst daring to live the life imagined; the real and true life our souls call us to. You all are amazing and have helped me continue to heal and grow just by walking with you. Thank you!

Thanks to little and big me for being my very own S/hero. For honouring my soul, my truth, my reason for *being*. Thank you to me for never giving up on myself and for tenaciously following inner promptings. So much to thank myself for! But, I will leave it here.

And last, but by no means least, I thank the Benevolent Life Powers That Spiritually Be in this world. I am over-joyed that it is You in charge and You that has the last word, however much we humans give all credit to ego and egocentric ways of living, being and seeing. Thank you Mother, Father, God, that is LOVE, for this much bigger picture that is over and above us all and is in All Ways, always good. So glad that I am - that we have been fashioned out of you and given all that we need, securely tucked within our hearts and soul, to re-discover at any time and make that ***all important journey*** back home to love and to all that has soul.

Foreword

Experience is a hard teacher because she gives the test first and the lesson afterwards.
- Vern Law

Experience Teaches.

Contents

Part Three: She Who Must Be and Can Never Be Turned.

Part Four: Full Cycle

Part Five: Unprecedented

Epilogue: On Being Human, Kind

Introduction

Sankofa is an African word from the Akan tribe in Ghana. The literal translation for the word and the symbol is "it is not taboo to fetch what is at risk of being left behind."

- Carter G. Woodson, 'The Mis-Education Of The Negro'

Sankofar is derived from the words: **SAN** (*return*), **KO** (*go*), **FA** (*look, seek and take*)

Visually and Symbolically, *Sankofa* is expressed as a mythic bird with its feet firmly planted forward with its head turned backwards. The Akan believe the past serves as a guide for planning the future and that there is wisdom in learning from the past which ensures a strong future.

For the Akan there must be movement and new learning as time passes.

Carter G. Woodson was an African-American scholar whose dedication to celebrating the historic contributions of Black people, led to the establishment of Black History Month which is marked every February in America since 1976, following suit in London, England, in 1987. Carter G. Woodson, in his ground-breaking book, 'The Mis-Education of the Negro', draws on the meaning and importance of *Sankofar* to help African people rediscover and reclaim back their true history and identity, as Historic Generational Identity theft had taken place.

In this body of my work, '**Inner Life Writes**', individual pieces of my writing speak on this *looking back* to **UN**-learn, **RE***-learn and* **RE***-turn to* who I truly am and move, more securely, towards *my purpose* in this world; the reason for our *being* here, and being here *truly*.

It has been thirty-six years since I made that Sankofa Braveheart move to go and get help for the psychological wounds I had incurred from a past that was my childhood. Past hurts, unprocessed, in need of being grieved and healed, enough that I may **RE**-new and **RE**-turn and *go/grow* on. It has been some journey, one that has included the healing of the racial trauma from the experience of being a Black African (Caribbean British-born) woman in this time. Generationally healing from the experience of slavery which, just like the loss of my childhood, continues to negatively impact today.

Black people today are still losing their lives at the destructive hands of the *'malignant powers that be'* laws. And the black child, by the age of 3 years old, has already swallowed wholesale Western society's unconscious envy, masked in hatred of his darker hue brothers and sisters, now internalised in the black child as *self-hatred*. Also known as Internalised Racism. The traumatic is set skin-deep.

Black people have been very much mis-educated against; an education in the Western world that feels more like a violence, like an experience of being *'done to'* as a race of people. It is very wise to understand this - this mis-education hurts us all! It hurts the world and its future livelihood. The cry of the Sankofa has never been so loud at this current time and in this current climate in the world. As Dr. Martin Luther King warns,

We must LEARN to live together as brothers, or we will perish together as fools.

So, from the healing-dream-making-journey I have been on, I have discovered my reason for being is to start with myself and dare to make that **RE**-turn for the sake of the planet, the love of my people, and the joy and fulfilment of my Soul. My Soul just loves that stuff! Just loves that kind of deep and true life and living.

Having **RE**-turned from the wreckage of my personal & collective past, arriving at my more psychologically, racially, spiritually liberated Self, I believe my purpose on this earth plane is to be a *Light-Giver and Bearer,* offering in the sharing of my Inner-sight, pearls of wisdom: lessons learned from The Great Wisdom School of *Learning from Experience to Progress and Move Forward.*

Like the Ancient Egyptian Goddess, *Maat,* I bring my heart to bear and weigh against the light of my most deep and true inner-outer life experience, coming from my Soul's unique perspective. I own these Inner Life **RE-***flections.* I own them totally and *soulfully,* knowing that how I see, we see, "the world" is filtered through our own individual experiences: one **REALity** many people to experience it, in unique diversity. Out of One, many.

The Critical Psychological and Philosophical Analysis IN-Sights/Her Says (Essays) shared here are raw, real, relevant and contemporary, filled with the wisdom gained from knowing myself *deeply,* from this learning and **RE**-turning, and learning and **RE**-turning some more. Some of the Essays/Her Says shared here are memoir-like, some teachings, some poetry. All very human and applicable to the human (felt) experience and condition. The Personal is universal as well as political.

I truly believe, as human beings, we have *that something inside so strong*, that InnerLight In-Sight, that can help us overcome almost anything and everything in this life, whilst holding steadfast to an unwavering love for humanity, in all its light forms.

This collection, and petition of and for opening more to Inner Life, are on subjects very close to my heart and the *Heart and Soul* of my healing, **RE**-Newal and **RE**-turn. Subject matters which us humans struggle & grapple with, which have reached fever pitch in the world again today. Yet, a critical mass has been building, especially off the back of the 2020 Pandemic that was, still is, and still has us reeling from, Covid. Michael Meade in his book, '*Awakening the Soul*', sums up most beautifully this **RE**-newing way of being & experiencing the world more lit and awake when he said,

> *In the course of Life, we must awaken to a greater Sense of Self or else become more isolated, divided and subject to increasing anxieties and feelings of helplessness and despair. The most common reason for despair and alienation comes from not being who we truly are at the Core of Our Souls. The human Soul, by its very nature, is ancient and resilient.*

I love that! I love that truth! Truth just *is*. IS-ness. Us humans need to IS-up!

I am, we are - black people especially are - living examples of this ancient resilience, especially on that Sankofa journey back from ambush, trauma and mis-education. That ground of truer being planted firmly in the root of **RE**-newal, now finds me living the life imagined... those most precious dreams secretly hidden. I am now living in the land of *The All That I May Be*, which provides safe passage to the effortless realisation of dreams. The dreams of good folks woke. I am also, amongst other things, the hope and the dream of ancestors once enslaved.

Having transformed- i.e. **RE-**turned to love's true shape & form, with clearer vision & aim of my life purpose & direction, many dreams on this road of true being have come through and true for me. This you will discover as you read.

To put out there, in way of disclaimer, my heartfelt Intention in this book is not to 'attack' and 'make people feel bad'. My Intention is to give those who need it, a good 'shake-up, wake-up' call, like an aggravated parent gives their child after numerous times of trying to wake them up for school. I believe we are being *called* in life at this time to wake up to our Personal and Collective responsibilities and life lessons - an education we will never acquire in schools where Western ideologies dominates and colours worldview.

True worldview includes us all. It includes all of our contributions on this world stage, still outstanding for African people today. But things are changing. Ready or not, shifts are taking place and it is my belief that we need to take our place in response.

The further away a society drifts from truth, the more it will hate those who speak it.

In regard to the above quote, we have historically bared witness to this truth. And some of us have even bared witness to this in our personal homes, especially in the proverbial experience of being casted 'black sheep'. If you have ever been called the black sheep of the family, that is indeed a compliment! Receive it as such.

Oftentimes, before the truth sets us free, it roughs us up somewhat. Expect that. I make no apologies for my stance on subjects close to the heart in this book. When Love says jump, I say, "how high?!" Not wishy-washy love. Love that stands and dies for something; that puts itself on the line for something.

To note, in this body of work, I emphasise the word **RE,** which was the name given in Ancient Egypt for the Sun God - the most important of Ancient Egyptian gods. **RE** was considered to be the King of the Gods. I use **RE** in my work to Signify **RE**-newal mostly, **RE**-turn especially and **back** to Love figuratively. Back to who we truly are and have been made to be and to come; a very unique and indi-vidual drop in the **BE**-longing ocean of the *Great I Am,* wrapped up in its awesome, one-of-a-kind, love.

I also use **RE** to mean Inner/light, aka Sun - that light sourced through us on earth as humans, humans that have soul.

In this world, during these times, we need more soul in our lives, our hearts, our affairs. Using and highlighting **RE,** I believe adds more power and healing potency to what is being said in this *Inner Life Writes* body of work. My healing journey began in 1986 when I was 21. This body of work, therefore, spans 36 years. Also note that these writings are in subject matter order, not chronological order.

Words have power and I honour that power here as the following poem I wrote in 2004 declares...

WORDS

I don't abuse Words,
or misuse Words; I use Words to
show and tell the truth of my being
and feelings - my Words are revealing,
sacred even, because in the beginning there was,
The Word.

And now, the pleasure it brings,
and how my soul sings to share
meaningful Holy Communication with you -
another who is true and uses Word Power to
inspire righteous truth.

So, let's get down to some good conversating
and together incarnate The Spaces wherein
our Words rings true, and reawakens
the innermost recess of you, me, us, we,
and in our resurrected rediscovery let's create
anew, by speaking affirmative Words into,

the Deeds we do, the Words we use,
the Thoughts that are pure, and all the more
re-presents you, fore as a people and a species
we have Nuff Work to do.

So, come. Join me on this healing and **RE**-membering Sankofa journey and passage back home to soul and to deeper and true living and being. Join me in the Inner Life underground, where I - as healed, healing and healer, like the Great Ms. Harriet Tubman - set souls free to be and to **BE**-come, all that they may be.

Let us roll back home to the personal and collective tree that feeds good and just living, allowing others their portion, similarly.

To quote Malcolm X...

"Sometimes a fruit falls from a tree and rolls so far away from its roots that it's no longer of the tree. The hard fall, and long journey, bruises the fruit so much that it totally changes it. It's the same way for some of our people. This is why some can't be awakened regardless of how much truth you present to them. This journey has totally brainwashed them to such a degree that they're no longer of the original tree."

Dream, but stay steadfast to Woke! The Tree of Life is meant to feed and grow us... all!

Be you, truly. Grow through what you go through, and *don't shade your shine*, as love very much minds!

Love and Light,

Denise James, September 2022

If you have come
to help me
you are wasting your time.
But, if you have come
because
your liberation
is bound up
with mine
then let us work
together.

- Lila Watson. Australian Indigenous, Elder, Activist & Educator

Part One: The Personal Historical

The Wise Innocent knows that our lives are defined not by what happens to us, but by how we think about what happens to us.

- Carol S. Pearson, The Hero Within

POEM: Taboo To-Boot

Can I talk of it here?
Hope you don't squirm in your chair and pretend
    not to hear...
I know it can be hard acknowledging someone
    else's pain - especially when yours is exactly
    the same.

How many of you have experienced childhood
    abuse -
physical, emotional, sexual too?
The great taboos we are most forbidden from
    disclosing,
especially if the abuse took place in our own
    houses.

Perhaps it was by thy mother or thy father;

an uncle, an aunt, a sister, a brother -
or some other family member or friend...
shall I go on? You say when.
Or then again, maybe it was all of the above,
the likes of which was carefully coated in sugar
    sweet love.

Child Abuse, the betrayal of betrayals,
shatters the soul, leaving great big gaping holes
in places that comes to feel it can never be filled,
creating areas in your being where you daren't let
    others in.

Not to mention the maddening silence
whereby you are expected to forever refrain
from ever speaking about it, therefore releasing the
    pain -
the price of which extinguishes your own flame.

And somewhere inside an essential part of you
    dies,
hidden, buried, abandoned, denied,
as you try to carry on and lead a so called 'normal
    life.'

Suffering so, secretly hating yourself,
where nothing feels real, or lasts for long,
and all good feelings are dead and gone.

To cope, you may have forgotten what happened
    to you;
for this you will never be true.
But, take heart, dear heart I am here to tell and
    share -
there are people out there who really do care.

You see, Your Soul can never be totally destroyed;
just realise that you can decide, at any given time,
to recreate Your Life. Such is the power
that lies within you: to Self-actualise and to thine
    own self, be true.

Give yourself another chance; embrace the all of
    which you are,
for despite the perpetrator's disgrace, it wasn't you
    who fell
from being an honourable member of the human
    race.

Refuse to give eyes to their why's and their lies
of their transgressions - *YOU WERE NEVER TO
    BLAME,*
it was their crime against you that made you a
    shame.

Strengthen your linking influence in the cycle
    of life

by fighting for Your Rights, making your spirit
    strong,
and daring to sing your own redemption song.

Honour that part of you that lies tattered and blue
and needs to be recovered, it's been long overdue.
Now is the time for resurrection -
for some kind of emotional and spiritual correction
    - don't you too pass the buck back down into
    generations.

Let's save the babies, our higher ideals,
by cherishing our children and teaching them how
    to be
real valuable members of the community.
Let's keep them near and dear to our hearts,
and do our very best to give them good starts,
so they won't come to be many times defeated in
    the race of life.

Cuddle them, talk to them, show them you care;
let them know, if all else fails,
you will always be there.
Teach them also, all that glitters is not gold -
don't leave them open to the draining and theft of
    their Souls.

And finally, before I go,

know this too -
You can't truly love someone
if you don't **love you.**

On Being A Survivor Of Childhood Trauma:
Survived

I am a Survivor; that I am. I am also Victim as that sense of brokenness lies at the centre of the Survivor within me. The two are intimately related, though somehow estranged. I am also neither Survivor nor Victim: *I Am Me,* the me I was before either of these.

I have found, out of all these selves, the world prefers my Survivor self and I have come to prefer her myself. The Victim oftentimes doesn't get a real look in; people find her hard to deal with, denying her instead, victimizing her all over again.

Having been in Survivor mode some 40 plus years, the Victim within has taken up certain residence. It has been a great big challenge letting her in and letting her be, as she seemed to go against the Survivor in me.

As for Me, Me doesn't know who she is and who she would like to be. Because Me wasn't around for very long before disaster struck, she doesn't quite know that she deserves good things. When it comes to allowing herself what she truly wants and needs, the Victim within makes Me feel worthless, like I am asking way too much, and that the good things others get to have is not for the likes of Me. Things like a more relaxed existence, a good marriage, meaningful work, a good income, supportive networks; to be allowed to follow My Bliss - whatever that is.

The Survivor in Me often overlooks both Victim's and Me's fears and vulnerabilities, wanting to *affirmation-away* every weakness, and continue forever forward and on, unaware of the toll of shouldering it all and soldiering on; carrying the world on my shoulders as if I am God and Archetypical Great Mother.

So next time you meet a Survivor of any sort, try to be compassionate and understand that beneath robustness oftentimes lives the Victim, and that well-being and recovery can be lifelong work. As can, very simply, being one's own and true Self.

Don't be quick to tell the Survivor to 'move on,' 'forgive' and not to 'dwell on the past', because that will most definitely be like rubbing salt in the wounds by telling Survivors it's their fault for taking however long the healing process needs, however well-intentioned you think your words to be.

Just listen, compassionately, however difficult that may be. Your being able to do so helps Survivors more than you will ever know. It helps us to see that we are not to blame; we are not alone. It helps us to know that we deserve good things and that we have all the time we need to heal and feel at home in this world that has not treated us well, especially when being treated well was critical to our development. These things Survivors needs to hear and understand, and I say again, so much more than you can know...

On Finding Your Voice:
Finding Voice

Quiet. That's what they called me whilst growing up. Quiet and shy with an ever-ready plastered-on smile... from the outside. Inside, I was quietly terrified; terrified of being laughed at and/or assaulted by ever-ready crashing words, by violating hands...

Quiet I was and quieter I got, until, in the end, I almost became invisible - one less problem to be dealt with. I got praise for being 'quiet' and 'good.' I put *a lot* of effort into being invisible.

I got so good at being quiet, that even when I needed to tell, I couldn't; I couldn't find the words. They were nowhere to be found.

I suffered in silence, no less.

A godsend to my abusers who I thought, at first, were being nice to me by giving me much needed attention, understanding I have needs to be taken care of...

EVERYTHING became so mixed up; so inside out.

I grew up and left childhood, feeling like I was never raised but drowned instead; feeling tricked and cheated, yet expected to get on with it- with the business of being adult - when all I felt inside was little, pretending to be big and unaffected by all that had passed. I guess sooner or later that shit was going to hit the fan.

It blows my mind that people don't get this. That they aren't able, or willing, to do the simple mathematics and understand that it's either I am going to take the unfinished business and unlearned lessons of childhood out on me, and/or on somebody else. Either way, recreating and repeating the history of pain.

Except the buck stopped with me - not accidentally, but by choice. By a choice I made just before I became a mother, therefore, automatically a teacher. Back then I promised myself to make a difference... A promise that continues to date, but a promise that is also lifelong work, as the damage done was so deeply set that undoing it initially felt like I was hurting myself.

It has been words that have saved me; searching for them and sharing them in therapy, through journaling, poems, and writing my life story, hoping one day it will be published... which it was. My first book **'Back to Love'** was published January 7th 2021.

I love words; they help me to have a say - to have MY say; to not be quiet about the things that, like cancer, if left untreated can kill... kill individuals, families, communities, nations...

We are all affected by injustice, wherever it is taking place. It blows my mind that people don't understand this, and feign shock, horror, surprise, when we read about another mindless killing of innocent lives in the papers...

There is a relationship between past and present; between cause and effect; there is no denying this. A seed is sown to avenge, and/or revenge, when someone has been done wrong. It must be worked out somehow and try to be made undone.

So, as long as I am here, I will have *My Say,* in the hope that somewhere those once silenced words, the quiet storm that I was, will make a difference, like how a pebble thrown into a pond makes ripples.

It is also my hope that the little difference I can make will go a very long way, for the greater good. This is how I choose to work through my unfinished business and, in doing so, sing the particular *Personal Truth Song* I believe my soul came to this earth plane to sing, and have heard. A sweet singing bird, uncaged.

On Mind-Body Balance:
Down

What I am going to talk about here is a going *Down* that happens when I ain't been around for myself; when I live upstairs in my head for too long.

I love living and being up there, playing with ideas, working at my dreams, reading books, honing my craft of true self-development and my life's work as a therapist helping to bring people back home to themselves; bringing them back to loving and appreciating themselves and honouring who they truly are, outside of the good opinions of others. I love all that, I do. The problem is that I can stay up there, in my head, way too long and to the extent that I get lost and, in the process, lose grounding in my body and contact with myself on that important level. I lose ground and a certain part of me gets *Down* because I ain't around; I'm missing in thought.

It gets so that I come to be way too far from home, like a young person who has been absent outdoors way past the time they have been allowed, and now they are afraid to come home and face the consequences. That's how it can get for me, and it does not help that historically and developmentally I was not taught to self-regulate and 'wind down' - there were no reliable adults at home or around to provide that much needed well-being life lesson. No responsible adults sufficiently at home within themselves, let alone at night-time or daytime, where in their company I could feel safe enough to trust going into that kind of restful slumber state. The world, especially at night-time, was not a safe enough place for me to relax and comfortably be with myself like that. Through no fault of my own, I missed that class.

I know my current ongoing struggle in this area of my life roots back there, but I need to address this area of difficulty as it is having a bearing on my well-being; its effects are spiralling, and I am not getting any younger. I still have adventures I want to experience so I need my health, strength and vitality, and this fear of coming *Down* needs to dissolve. Not being able to relax and let go is taking a toll on my moods and my relationship with food, not to mention what goes on in the crazy world of being peri-menopausal.

With regard to my relationship with food, I am an emotional eater, and, because of a certain past, food took on magical powers in my impressionable young mind years ago; the magical power of giving my days focus, therefore, helping me try to overlook the miserable turns my childhood lanes took. The magical power of having something potentially nurturing and nourishing to look forward to, especially waking in the mornings and arriving back into an uncared for reality. The magical power of anaesthetising painful troubled feelings whenever tasty food treats and I were in each other's company, momentarily hit *The Emptiness Spot*. As a little girl I so loved my sweets! As a child I couldn't quite get enough of it... like now with my sugary teas.

As an adult, I want to emotionally eat when I am tired and finding it ever so hard to *wind down* and take that much needed rest of an evening, becoming instead like a visibly tired child who feverishly fights sleep not wanting the day to end but stay up and see, 'What else?' "What next?" Additionally, I tend to want to emotionally overeat when I have taken on too much and given out too much emotional energy, attempting to make it up to myself with a tasty treat, much like a busy and tired mummy tries to distract and pacify her child with sweets and all manner of things, when all her child truly needs is her good company. Like that busy mummy, in place of giving that special time to myself, I give that part of me delicious food treats instead.

I read on social media the other day:

Stop the glorification of busy.

Very true that.

Yes, bills need to be paid, but equally, and now I unceasingly believe more importantly, Inner lights need to shine; lives need to be lived and be lived to one's fullest. Well, my life does anyway. It's in my genes; I can't shake it. So, I need to face and learn the *coming down back to ground* life lesson and live my life in more *body-mind balance.*

On Finding Rest In The World:
Home Is Where The Heart Is

Today I am much less a stranger in my body. This is still very much work in progress for me, added to the ongoing effort to acquire a more restful heart, as the quote below reminds me:

> *A heart that has learned to trust can be at rest in the world...*
>
> *Home is where the Heart Is.*

I became a stranger in my body quite early on and, when life got really bad, I came to see my body as the 'enemy,' especially when it wouldn't listen to me and not *feel*. Things became very mixed up real quick.

Now, as an adult, I'm trying to turn that around but it is so hard. It's like an untrained person having to completely pull down an old house and build it back up with new materials; carrying out all of the re-wiring and learning everything solely by trial and error. Causing a few explosions here and there; fearing you are going to die at times. Fighting fatigue, but never giving up because you have come too far, and you need light for the dark, so you don't have to live anymore in so much fear. This is what the process of feeling more at home in my body has come to be and feel like for me.

Trying to see my body as 'friendly' is ongoing work. I am still very much at the rewiring stage, and I am learning to accept that this may be lifelong work. And what makes it all such a huge mountain to climb? The faulty wiring happened during my most formative, vulnerable and impressionable years, with no loving, protecting, nurturing adult to oversee and ensure the right wiring was firmly rooted in place.

So now, as an adult in the healing process, when I try to turn it all back around, an alarm bell goes off and I think I am being broken into - that I am in actual danger; that my body, my feelings, my sensations are out of control and that everything is working against me. When all that is happening is that I am coming home into being more fully human, full of breath, depth and inside-out Presence.

Lively and independent thinking children and adults can be seen as a problem to societal 'social order,' as I at times perceive my lively body to be. My anxiety has risen since I am living more complete in my body - still at times a stranger to myself, and at other unexpected times, the love of my life. Self-love is a beautiful thing; I am coming to know and feel that which makes all the hard work worth it.

So, I will work on my castle of love for as long as is needed, creating new beginnings, and finishing this life journey dissimilar to how my life originally started. This, I promise to myself, because just like a house is not a home without love in it, I cannot feel at home in my body without being in it... **home is where the heart is.**

On Growing Up Sooner
Than Humans Are
Wired For:
Lap-time

Laptime was a word coined in the 90's by Dr. Frances
Cress Welsing in 'The Cress Theory of Color-Confrontation and Racism'. I first heard the term Laptime encapsu-
lated in her ground-breaking book 'The ISIS Papers, The
Keys To The Colors.'

Dr. Frances Welsing was an American Afrocentric Psychi-
atrist and in her book symbolically drew upon the story of
the well-loved and revered Egyptian Goddess Isis. For
your information, the name Isis is a Greek corruption -
Egyptian hieroglyphics only recorded consonants and
omitted vowels, therefore, the true Egyptian pronuncia-
tion is unknown.

Isis was one of the main characters of the Osiris myth, in
which she resurrects her slain husband, the divine king,
Osiris, and produces and protects his heir, Horus. She was
believed to help the dead enter the Afterlife as she had

helped Osiris, and she was considered the divine mother of the Pharaoh, who was likened to Horus. A truly restorative and healing story, especially for black folks in these times, with man's continuing inhumanity to man - an inhumanity that very much includes himself seen as we are all members of the one human race, irrespective of our differences and physical appearances.

Dr. Frances Cress Welsing used the term *Laptime* when she was talking about young people becoming sexually active before they are psychologically ready to be, least of all being grown to raise to the challenge of being parents. Many of these children came from poverty - stricken inner cities - and she argued that what these young people were seeking in such relationships was not sex per se, but comfort, security, protection, home, love. They were seeking that which they were not getting enough of at home, which all children need for optimal human development; much like a plant will lend itself to being bent out of shape to find and receive the daylight and nourishment it needs, which has been placed out of reach. Such is the life-force within living things.

Laptime depicts regular quality time spent on parents'/caregivers' laps, in love's presence, feeling body-to-body warmth. In those moments, feeling safe and secure which is a much needed buffer, as well as little piece of heaven, in a hostile world. It is as important to humankind as food is to the body to eat.

Houses must have loving, caring, present and aware people living in them to make them mostly happy homes. I was one of those emotionally (and otherwise) deprived inner city children, who constantly longed for the warmth provided by being in close proximity to another warm-bloodied soul.

I too had been terribly starved in these quarters. I do not recall any Laptime. That deprivation was the motivating force behind my decision to have a child at 17 years old. I desperately wanted to give, and have my love received, by another human being. I wanted and needed to know how that felt. I wanted and needed to know what difference that would make to human life, not having experienced much of it myself. This is also one of the reasons why I am a counsellor today. I remember clearly making that decision at the age of 21 years old, when I put myself into therapy and experienced the healing power of being *given to and mirrored* in that special, gentle, and attentive way. The experience made me want to be in the position to give that gift of emotional presence, nourishment and nurturance to others in need.

Whilst reading Dr. Frances Cress Welsing's book in the 90's, the concept of Laptime helped me to see the unmet need behind young people engaging in grown up activities, not having been children for long. It helped, and still helps me, to take the judgement out of those kinds of psychosocial situations; it helps take the judgement out of external appearances of what could be, and are oftentimes, deemed as very poor choice.

At this present time, and as an adult, I've been needing some Laptime. Time out of my mind where I come down, and ground, after being out in the rat race and engaging in adult things for too long. I need Laptime so I can spend good, quality, restorative time with myself, centred at home inside my body, close to an Inner Silent Source and Knowing, that sustains & comforts me...

This coming down time does not come easy for me, as this emotional self-regulation was never passed down and I never learned from my caregivers at the opportune childhood time. Laptime, aka self-care, for me is life's work - a work very much in progress. However, I will give myself props, because in this area I have come a very long way. I am much better at being with myself and feeling the sweet comfort in doing nothing - just simply being. Being in the moment and smelling the rose of *in the greater scheme of things, all is very well,* of which I am eternally grateful, given those meagre beginnings...

Learning to stop often for Laptime, where nothing is taken for granted, and the whole of me rejoices in good-enough being, is a blessing; a blessing I make time to embrace whenever my mind is empty-enough of its contents, to fully receive the *Amazing Grace of Presence*: Presence of mind, Presence of heart, Presence of being.

This Laptime, like the Goddess Isis, brings mind, body and soul back into a unified whole, restored and preciously held, in its One True Self. The One the Lord looked back on and is well pleased with.

So, be still and know... You are loved, as you are. No need to run away and deny yourself. Be the blessing you already are by simply **being here.** And, metaphorically, climb on your lap from time to time for some much-needed restorative *me time.*

On Needing & Being Without True Refuge:

Who Will Cry For The Little Black Boy?

'Who will Cry For The Little Boy' is a poem written by Antwone Fisher, whose life story healing journey book 'Finding Fish' was made into a film directed by and starring Denzel Washington. A life marred by deprivation, child physical, sexual and emotional abuse, Antwone Fisher did not allow those enormous psychological injuries to fully determine his life's Journey.

It is a poignant poem for our wounded youths at this time - those who go on to hurt through their hurt, and those who are able to turn hurt into healing, hope and difference-making.

I will cry for the little black boy; I do cry for the little black boy, and the little black girl, all around the world, living in the absence of loving and protective childhood environments; in a society that can do so much better for and by them. I cry for them all, and for those little children inside grown people whatever race, colour or creed. Young people are our vulnerable of vulnerables, for which we are responsible.

It takes a village, people!

Let us not allow the (material world) struggle to become our identity. We are more than what 'happens' to us; more than what people think of us, and more than we have come to believe we are. We are basically good to the core, given a real, a true, a fair, shot at life, and given places and spaces where we can let our Inner life lights more truth-fully and fully shine. With Love, all things are indeed possible, as this following poem testifies to...

POEM: Mother Lover

Back in The Day we lived large,
played hard - unconditionally loved
by the Great Mother; Self-loving in Her Nature.

Then it came to pass,
a mean spirited, player hating, cold chill farce
held Her Sons to ransom; claimed Her, then
    raped Her.

Now Her sweet Sons don't shine like before,
their throats are sore, from the pressure she
    applied
to hold them back, until such time
Vision was restored.

And as time passes by, memory fades;
whilst some of Her Sons still re-members

The Day, others buckle under the mental health
     strain;

Some becoming more like Gangcesters,
dis-membering, everything, both big and small
that resembles themselves at all.

But Her Love is Pure, She both under and over
     stands
that the rage like fire burns strong
and is still in need of being undone,

So Her offspring's may sing
a more reparative redemption song
and like Eagles fly East-Homeward bound;
forward out of this, Babylon.

And then, The Right Time Come,
and the Grand Mother bawl – "Fire a ga bun!
Go get 'em Son! Regain your rightful positions!"

And with nuff love ina dem Hearts,
Her Truth upon their Tongues, their Quest?
To cut away all falsehoods from this-
Her kingdom.

So, "Fret not yourself my brothers",
The Mother Loves us ever so much,
and as a Matter of Cause, is oh so Desirous of us

to find **The Will to Live and Love.**

So Remember, as it was in the beginning
So we shall be in the end; Her Sons Shining,
like the Phoenix Forever Raising -
again and again and again.

On Complex Trauma:
Post-Traumatic Stress Disorder & Gang Violence

With all the talk on knife and gun crime amongst young black people, nothing is being said about the possible, and probable, cases of *Post-Traumatic Stress Disorder* (PTSD) arising from the impact of gang violence in inner cities. PTSD is not just a probability experienced by young people active in gangs, but also by people living in those areas trying to go about their everyday businesses and lives. Not taking into account the assault on mental health and well-being of young people not involved in gang violence, as well as on mothers, fathers, other family members and friends of those killed and/or assaulted: all inadvertently becoming victims of gang violence themselves.

As a mother of two black men and a grandmother of grandsons, their safety is a daily concern for me, especially when they are out and about in the world. That concern had already been there, though more centred around my fears of possible (and some would say probable) run-ins with the law, and other 'powers that discriminatory be.' Additionally, I can struggle with anxiety, so this ongoing climate of youth violence oftentimes compounds my own anxiety, which must also be the case for those already living with mental health concerns at this time. Therefore, one does not need to be affiliated to gangs to be affected by it and feel terrorised by it, living in these kinds of inner-city war zones.

Then there is the *Direct Trauma* which is experienced when witnessing a young person being harmed and/or losing their life, as well as the mental health assault of bereavement when one experiences the loss of lives of friends and loved ones. As is already well known, bereavement has its own special effects and process of grief, which is far from easy. I can put money on it, that out of those impacted, in whatever fashion, very few are in receipt of counselling and, therefore, end up dragging all that unprocessed and unresolved trauma into adulthood, and across generations. And so, the devastation goes on.

Then there is *Complex Trauma* which is very debilitating, even more so when it is added into the mix of gang violence. A type of trauma that still has not received the recognition it is due. This kind of trauma comes from having experienced abuse during one's childhood; in this situation the trauma very much shapes you, whether you believe it does or not. It shapes you deeply and physiologically when the abuse is experienced at the hands of family friends and/or loved ones themselves - the very people who are meant to be there to love and protect you. This kind of early ongoing and personality shaping Complex Trauma is also far more complex, though far from impossible, to treat.

It is indeed a very sad reality that it is not the 'stranger' who oftentimes presents the danger to children; the threat is on the doorstep in children's homes. The danger is in the place the child is meant to feel safe. It is of no surprise, to me anyway, that for some children it is the gangs that can come to feel more like home - more like a place where they feel protected, can gain a sense of belonging and acceptance, and receive some level of caretaking. Although, the cost of that is oftentimes immense.

Let's take a look at some statistics:

Over 51, 000 children in England were identified as needing protection from abuse in 2017, (The National Society for the Prevention of Cruelty to Children (NSPCC); 90% of sexually abused children were abused by someone they knew, (The National Association for People Abused in Childhood (NAPAC); 1 in 4 adults, males and females, would have experienced some form of sexual abuse by the time they are 18 years old: 1 in 4 girls and 1 in 8 boys.

And to further make mention, there is no hierarchy in child abuse. Neglect, physical, sexual, emotional, verbal, bullying and online abuse, are all forms of child abuse and are equally damaging in and of themselves. With particular regard to mental health, 1 in 4 people will experience a mental health problem in any given year, and 1 in 10 young people will experience mental health problem, which oftentimes gets mistaken for run of the mill 'teenage angst.'

Then there is the societal tendency for young black males aged 18-25 years old to be diagnosed with a psychotic mental health disorder. On the one hand, this is suspicious because the statistic is marked and unchanging, but, on the other hand, it is of no surprise when we seriously consider all the variables I am bringing to attention here. To me, it is not rocket science why people from black communities in general do not access counselling and other types of preventative services. Why instead, black people mostly present at crisis points, and are over-represented in youth juvenile systems, prisons, social services, mental hospitals, and so on.

Considering the impact on the economy, a study carried out in England in 2010, found that mental illness alone cost the economy £105.2 billion. In spite of this figure, mental illness is still under-recognised and under-treated in primary care.

Let us now take a look at physical health and well-being. The Adverse Childhood Experience (ACE) Study, (retrieved 25 March 2014, a research study conducted by

Kaiser Permanente Health Maintenance Organisation and Centres for Disease Control and Prevention), well documents Adverse Childhood Experiences on adult physical health. The types of childhood trauma associated with adult high risk health behaviours, such as smoking, alcohol and drug abuse, promiscuity, and severe obesity, and correlated with ill-health including depression, heart disease, cancer, chronic lung disease and shortened life span, are physical abuse, sexual abuse, emotional abuse, physical neglect, emotional neglect, mother treated violently, household substance abuse, household mental illness, parental separation or divorce and an incarcerated household member.

Having gathered up these very telling social facts, and with the emphasis on Control and Prevention, the authors also identified trauma-informed and resilience-building practises based on the research that is being implanted in communities, education, public health departments, social services, faith –based organisations and criminal law in America. We too on these sides of the world shores can benefit from drawing some important lessons of our own from pieces of research such as these, especially around control and prevention.

Indeed, Britain has started to make little headway. For example, regarding domestic violence and abuse, some lessons have been drawn from similar types of studies in Britain and are currently trying to be addressed in a primary care training and support programme called Identification and Referral to Improve Safety (IRIS, Ran by Queen Mary University of London, 2007-2010) IRIS is a collaboration between primary care and third sector organisations specialising in Domestic Violence and Abuse. A GP, on IRIS trained practise, has been quoted as saying:

"I'm now convinced that violence against women and children is a major public health problem with long-term consequences for women and their families. As an experienced GP, the whole project has been nothing short of transformational."

More needs to be documented and disseminated to all the key players in the Primary and Social Health Care fields – as well made available for the general population on the issue of Complex/PSTD. More needs to be said and disseminated on Mental and Physical ill-health that surrounds, and is also coming out of, inner city gang violence, highlighting the social conditions that compound these problems, namely poverty, discrimination, deprivation, racism, and Adverse Childhood Experience.

Hate yourself in the morning of your life, and by afternoon time you will be hating everyone else.

With regards to treatment in the way of medication, yes, it is not the sole source of help, but it absolutely has its place. It has its place when treating PTSD and other enduring Mental Health conditions, those that have become more ingrained, out of hand, and are havocking dire consequence on the person's day to day life. But, for true recovery, which benefits the individual, the community, society, and the economy on a whole, medication should be used in conjunction with therapy. With that combination, oftentimes, the need for medication lessens and people can be weaned off it over time. Once the trauma that has brought on the unbearable symptoms has been psychologically processed and satisfactorily physiologically regulated, one's life can take a more productive and progressive turn and head in a happier and more wholesome direction.

I have come to know quite a bit on this subject of PTSD and Mental Health. Firstly from my own experiences, as well as in my work as a counsellor with women who have experienced historic and adult sexual and domestic violence. I have seen first-hand the impact of those traumas on mental health, well-being, relationships and self-esteem. To spell out more clearly, here are some of the symptoms of PTSD:

- **Sleep Disturbances** like nightmares and difficulties in falling asleep and staying asleep.
- **Flashbacks** triggered by smells, associated memories, certain situations, almost anything.

- **Intrusive Ruminating Thoughts** that one feels that they cannot switch off from.
- **Anxiety, Panic Attacks, Depression, Suicide, Suicidal ideation.**
- **Anger** turned outward against others, and/or inwards resulting in violence towards oneself, e.g. suicide, self-harm. Women tend to turn anger in on themselves, and men, outside of themselves.
- **Hyper vigilance,** feeling always on edge, unable to relax. Jumpiness. Dislike of loud unexpected noise.
- **Paranoia,** which with regard to gang violence can have some base in the reality of young people feeling unsafe in their communities; some feeling they need to carry guns and/or knives to protect themselves.
- **Agoraphobia,** a fear of venturing outdoors.
- **Substance Abuse, Alcohol Abuse and Eating Disorders, Self-harm, promiscuity,** in an attempt at self and emotional regulation, as well as a way to self-medicate, numb and escape the tortuous pain.

These PTSD symptoms and ways of coping are very real, as well as life-limiting.

To conclude, I am hoping that you can begin to see how incredibly complex this issue of gang violence is and how very important it is that solutions to end gang violence come from all psycho-social angles. Let us not waste time splitting hairs about the cause, but instead focus more on effective solutions. We have no time for scorekeeping and finger-pointing: it is distracting and time wasting. We need to simply try everything and see which solutions work best.

The issue of gang violence, and the immediate and far-reaching destruction it creates and leaves us with in its wake, does not need knee-jerk reactions and short-sighted opinions - it's deep. It needs to be approached from the grass root up, then travel back down again to make sure that what the grass root has said has been fully heard and taken into serious consideration. Then, off we all go to implement, from the grass root up and back down again, monitoring and evaluating failures and successes.

This gang violence will be a slow, although steady and certain, resolve. Far from a 'peanut throwing sprint,' which has oftentimes been the case with issues such as these, hence why not much has changed and things have steadily gotten worse. What is being called for, across the human condition board, is a life-change from us all. We all need to consistently take care of matters from our own end, then any place else we able to offer help: no more, no less. We, as a people, also need to have love and care for each other. A lot of outside forces work against us achieving this love and care for each other. The powers that destructively be, long time worked out and institutionalised, black folks' disunity, from the time of slavery, especially between the sexes. It is going to take on-going daily effort to undo this.

And bless you one and all; *You* who are already out there making a difference. A dark place in the world lights up because of your efforts, so do not underestimate the power and importance of your difference-making and much-needed contributions.

PSALM: My One Life

PSALM ONE

1. Imprisoned in a cage
under the lock and key
of another's rage.
2. Cold, huddled, forlorn, in
A desolate place, alone,
3. but somehow, I know,
what was done in the dark
will come to Certain Light,
and all will be made right.
Learning to fall
So that I may fly;
Apple of
The Father's Eye.

PSALM TWO

4. New hope comes along
in the role of being a mum.
5. Mother and child are one;
Certain conditions undone,
though happy families end
before long.
6. Starting all over again is
going to be tough, but
we're going to make it,
I am somehow sure on that!
Learning to fall
So that I may fly;
Apple of
The Father's Eye.

PSALM THREE

7. Through a Growing Faith
I begin to believe in myself;
going back to school;
heeding The Call to Counsel.
8. Then, The Joy of Graduation
confirms, with Your Kind of Love,
I truly Can!
9. I can do anything I set
My Mind to, as with You

All things are possible.
Learning to fall
So that I may fly;
Apple of
The Father's Eye.

PSALM FOUR

10. Rediscovering The One true self,
making many and further a change.
11. My house is more
My Home,
a place of Welcome,
Vibrancy, Warmth.
12. As my True Colours
Comes shining through;
13. Opening More
To The Power
Of You...
In Me.
Set Free.
Learning to fall
So that I may fly;
Apple of
The Father's Eye.

POEM: Secret Centre

In the Spring
there is Winter,
Resting.
In the Day-Light
there is Night-Time,
Patiently Awaiting.
In my Low and High drives
there is,
At All Times,
The Inner Me,
Secretly Marvelling
IN-
despite injustice -
Each and Every
Moment Of Being
In
Existence!

Part Two: Psyche-Social

Buddha taught that social institutions co-arise with us. They are not independent structures separate from our inner lives, like some backdrop to our personal dramas, against which we can display our virtues of courage and compassion. As institutionalised forms of our ignorance, fears and greed, they acquire their own dynamics. Self and society are both real, and mutually causative.

- Joanna Macy, 'World as Lover, World As Self'

POEM: God Bless The Child

The child within, a gift therein that
has been since the beginning of our time-
before you, we, us
became an I.

The child's eyes sees far and wide;
if you let it be your guide, it's wise sunshine
will make you smile.

For the child is both old and young,
a true champion that can make you feel, instantly
revitalised and undone.

So, if your child inside lies wounded, denied,
in a shame that binds,
heal its pain and regain recognition
through its wonder-filled fountain of youth -

patiently awaiting inside of you.

For you can't enter self-love's glorious kingdom
until you first come to be
As little children.

That's why the man's dem so vex,
that a gift so heaven sent,
weren't taught to love and respect itself-
And as some wise soul once said,

Hate yourself in the morning of your life
And by afternoon time, you'll be hating
  everyone else.

So, who God bless, let no man curse-
and God most definitely blessed, The Child,
so let us learn to do and be, like-wise.

On Healing From Trauma:
Trauma and Recovery

At the age of 21, I experienced a nervous breakdown. The Life Event precipitating that was the mentally and emotionally abusive relationship I was in. The desire to create my own 'happy family,' coming from a very broken one, had begun to crumble, which was psychologically devastating to me. During this time of having to face how bad for my mental wellbeing the relationship was, I began to experience a nervous breakdown: my eating disorder (I had been Bulimic since 14 years old) became more and more out of control; my thought processes began to break down - I couldn't think straight or stop myself from thinking when thinking became too much. My sleeping was disturbed night after night as I would dream of my partner treating me even more despicably than he did in waking life. It became a truly mentally tormenting time for me, enough to force me to go to the doctor as I feared that I was losing my mind. It took everything to make and keep that appointment.

After listening to me and asking questions, the doctor said that it sounded like I was having a nervous breakdown and that I was depressed. He prescribed antidepressants, sleeping tablets and suggested rest.

When I left the doctor's office, I felt an inner jubilance - there was something wrong with me and it had a name! 'Nervous Breakdown,' 'Depression.'

There begun my healing journey.

I didn't take the prescribed medications for long - maybe a week and a half; for me, at the time, I felt that tablets weren't going to make me well. Instead, a week following going to see my GP, I came upon an article on eating disorders and discovered that there was a name for what I did with food too, 'Bulimia' (I had felt too ashamed to tell the doctor about the eating disorder). I contacted the organisation who, at the bottom of the article, they suggested to go to for help.

Very many years of individual, as well as group, therapy followed - I learned that early experiences had traumatised me and had had a bearing on my emotional development, symptom formations (previously mentioned) and ongoing life struggles. From the experience of psychotherapy, significant positive life changes began to take shape, *inside-out.*

My story, and the development of multiple mental health conditions (an eating disorder, anxiety, depression), resembles the stories and symptom formation of the clients I have worked with. My clients and I experienced a *maladaptation* at a critical time in our development as children. This led to the development of a self-concept externally located. For myself, I had to be the strong, needless, ask-for-nothing little girl. I became a people pleaser and a great selfless understanding nurturer to everyone... my mother included. Indeed, in that sense my mother was my first child.

For my client KC, who I saw for counselling at The Rape Crisis Counselling Service I worked at, she developed a similar persona. Our sense of worth came from outside ourselves and from how others wished us to be and behave because of their own inabilities in the meeting of our developmental needs. This maladaptation comes at a great cost; the cost of losing our true self, our authentic self, and its innate unlimited potentiality. As we became lost to ourselves, a state of non-being cuts deep and sets in motion future difficulties and dis-ease, especially in relationships and the creation of unwholesome relationship patterns. Add into that, for both myself and other clients I have worked with, the trauma of childhood sexual abuse, emotional abuse, neglect, and abandonment, the stage truly becomes set for future mental health challenges.

For KC, having grown up in the daily warzone environment that is domestic violence and having a mother who was very depressed and would threaten to slash her wrists in front of her children, when she presented as a survivor of sexual violence as an adult by a family member, *mental health symptom formation* came to a head, along with *Post Traumatic Stress Disorder* (*PTSD*). And when her mother's alcohol abuse killed her, KC's alcohol consumption became problematic directly following.

Regarding the question, *'What is mental health?'* the World Health Organisation defines it as,

"Mental Health is a state of well-being in which every individual realises his or her own potential, can cope with the normal stresses of life, can work productively and fruitfully, and is able to make a contribution to her or his community"

I very much like the following definition of mental health:

"Mental Health is the emotional and spiritual resilience which enables us to enjoy life and to survive pain, disap-

pointment and sadness. It is a positive sense of wellbeing and an underlying belief in our own and others' dignity and self-worth'

- (HEA 1998)

Some myths and facts about mental health:

- Mental health problems are very rare; Fact: 1 in 4 people will experience a mental problem in any given year.
- People with mental illness aren't able to work; Fact: we probably all work with someone experiencing a mental health problem.
- Young people just go through ups and downs as part of puberty; Fact: 1 in 10 young people will experience a mental health problem.
- People with mental health illnesses are usually violent and unpredictable; Fact: people with mental illnesses are more likely to be a victim of violence.
- People with mental health problems don't experience discrimination; Fact: 9 out of 10 people with mental health problems experience stigma and discrimination...
- 1 in 4 people will experience mental ill health at some point in their lives through such life events as the break-up of a relationship, the loss of a

61

loved one, a job, children leaving home, a single traumatic event, historical child abuse, etc. Anxiety and depression are the most common mental disorder in Britain, with women being more likely to have been treated for a mental health problem than men. Depression also affects 1 in 5 older people.

(Mental Health Foundation, Registered Charity No. England 801130)

Mental health affects us all regardless of age, background, ethnicity, gender and class.

During our work together, KC attempted suicide. The suicide attempt was triggered by a very intense panic attack following an unexpected and unplanned encounter with her alleged perpetrator. During the panic attack (and trigger) KC experienced symptoms of intense fear; feelings of imminent danger and doom, the need to escape, palpitations, trembling, shortness of breath, chest pain, and the fear of dying.

We explored the suicide attempt in detail, the whole experience, from beginning to end, in order to bring the implicit feelings/material closer to the surface for KC to experience, process and understand in the safety of the therapeutic relationship. It became apparent that in her suicide attempt, KC was wanting to end the intense feelings and impending danger she felt. It had all felt too much in that moment. Unconsciously, she was thinking *'If I am in grave danger from something/someone 'out there,' this time I will have control; I will hurt myself. I can end it all.'*

Working with KC in a psychodynamic way was not only to bring insight in regard to her behaviour/responses when triggered and the situations and persons who trigger the PTSD response, but also to help in the work of considering and employing more healthy coping strategies - other than the one of hurting herself. I worked very closely with my supervisor around this incident and put in place with KC a **Safety Plan.** The Safety Plan document outlines a list of actions and reminders, created with clients, for the purpose of seriously re-thinking suicide and passing more safely through the difficult period, unharmed.

I believe that due to the very focused *reparative therapeutic work* KC and I did together in sessions following the suicide attempt, KC was able to make a different decision the next time she was triggered and felt suicidal. This was evidenced in a much later session, when KC discussed having experienced the same symptoms in relation to another situation involving her perpetrator. In spite of the thought to kill herself (to kill the awful feelings), KC pushed through her shame and embarrassment at feeling so panic stricken and in need of help, and called her father and sister for help. She also took herself to A & E.

During the course of therapy, as KC began to make more and more wholesome self-care judgements, coming from a more engaged and established internalised locus of evaluation (more *self*-rather than *other*-directed), she also owned her right to set healthy boundaries. Specifically, KC considered whether or not to see her perpetrator brother, opting for not in the end, when previously, KC had experienced intense inner conflict and guilt thinking about making this decision, being once so maladaptive, trauma bonded, and people-pleasing.

Another turning point in the counselling process working with self-worth, came in the way of the self-autonomous decision KC made to go on medication. We had spent time exploring her feelings and anxieties surrounding that decision, as well as external societal stigmas. In the end KC made the decision to opt for medication, mainly to help alleviate the PTSD symptoms which she felt were throwing her off course and getting in the way of progress, feeling so vulnerable, fragile, and easily triggered.

With regards to the development of mental and physical ill health following early traumatic experiences, studies like the *Adverse Childhood Experience Study* (*ACE*), has helped to shed important light on the matter. The ACE Study well-documents the relationship between past and present on adult mental and physical health. With the emphasis on Control and Prevention, the authors identify trauma-informed and resilience-building practises based on the research.

Resilience-building is a very important part of the work which counsellors do, i.e. helping clients build on any existing resilience already present in their psychological make-up and survival repertoire, and supporting the development of new, more life-affirming and enduring, coping strategies.

Through the establishment of a good working alliance and the development of a trusting bond in the therapeutic relationship, as a counsellor, I also use psycho-education to help build up cognitive resilience in the understanding of trauma and its recovery.

Building resilience in the trauma work I conduct, extends to 'body work and awareness'; the kind of body awareness Van der Kolk (1995) talks extensively about in his work with trauma and recovery, captured in the following quote,

"We remember less in words and more with our feelings and in our bodies"

For anyone reading this, thinking about KC's alleged rapist and wondering if she went on to press charges, one thing counsellors are not permitted to do is to tell clients what to do. *Decisions are their's alone.* Lots of the counselling space can be given to exploring all aspects of pressing criminal charges, but final decisions rest with the client.

To date, I have worked with a number of clients who have made the decision to press charges and, in seeing their plight and treatment (even with them being victim), I know for sure that one would have to have a certain amount of resilience and have carried out enough psychological healing and recovery to take on this challenge. A challenge that oftentimes, for whatever reason, does not even get the go ahead to go to court by the Crown Prosecution and, for those that do, justice is not very often easily served there.

For the full story of my own healing journey from Adverse Childhood Experiences, see my book, **'Back To Love'**, published 7th January 2021.

On Inner Life Connection:
In Deep

Bare skinned - yet totally complete,
Is how we First Entered In -
To Being,
later on becoming
multi-layered in, the many varied 'things,'
as we learned the words 'fit in.'

Whilst all the while **RE**-membering...
The Deep Peace With
IN
A Super-Natural Skin,
that's Soft, Yet *True Self-determining.*

Forever More
I Will Be
Emptying, Surrendering, Unburdening,

Whilst Awakening to
A Wise and Wonderful,
Winged Spirit Skin-Deep Within
That Knows How To
Sweep Itself Back
Into Completion in
Planet Earth Existence.

On Questions:

Quest-eons

A friend posed this question recently,

"If someone was abused in childhood, does that mean that person will grow up and abuse children similarly?"

My response..

This is the million-dollar question, and one that considers the argument of **nature verses nurture.** The paradox is that most perpetrators of childhood abuse have been abused in their childhoods, however, most people who have been abused in childhood don't go on to perpetrate abuse.

It is one of those questions that cannot be completely answered one way or the other. Well, not currently with the information we have at personal and collective human hand. Certain answers have been vehemently put forward from the main schools of thought: religion, psychology, biology, sociology, criminology, New Age etc. In my opinion, none of these responses have all the answers, which keeps the answer to this key question currently outside of human comprehension. Very often, the answer is 'a bit of this and a bit of that', as well as some (currently) unknown other thing. However, we human beings tend to like neatly packaged answers, with no wiggle room for uncertainty and new developments.

Yet, the wonderful thing about questions is that they set us off on missions, journeys, quests; it is as wise souls gone by have said, the question itself already holds the answer; like a mother carrying the seed of a soon-to-be-born baby, destined to be a child, and one day adult in the Life Cycle. This wisdom shows and tells us that if one has come to the question, if one has formed it in consciousness, the answer has, in that moment, been found, and now, patiently awaits being discovered. A discovery that may take aeons, but has been set in motion, nonetheless.

I think the question of repeating child abuse if one has been abused themselves is a question, just like the question of cancer, that need to be continually researched and explored because, like cancer, child abuse kills and its destructiveness spreads very far and very wide and across generations. I am at a place in life where I am always learning and informing myself, especially on the topic of human behaviour, growth, and development, especially when trauma has taken place. And today, I am very glad that I can now also peacefully live with the *yet to be more fully known in life,* that is oftentimes labelled uncertainty and fear of the unknown, when the unknown is just an **empty space yet to be filled**.... which is just rich fertile soil that, in our short-sightedness, we fill with all manner of fearful thought-filled things.

The fact that there is this paradox that most people who have been abused in childhood do not go on to abuse children themselves, gives me a lot of hope and continues to inform my belief that, at their core, the human being, upon entry into this world and parented and loved to a decent extent, is basically good at heart. It is what we do with the impressionable child and the child's impressionable mind- what we show him and her, as well as the kind of world, community, society, environment, and generational legacy that the human being is born into- that shapes and further informs the budding human spirit, for better and/or for worse.

There is this wonderful thing called **Self-Awareness,** interchangeably and sometimes referred to as **Agency,** that embraces 'difference-making'; the kind that aims to overturn unbalanced negatives into life-affirming positives. And there is also this mysterious, powerful, spiritually and emotionally nourishing thing called love, that undoes much and gives life that qualitative and creative Midas touch. Love has so many well-being, well-meaning and well-doing inner-side-out relatives, like Empathy, Peace, Truth and Joy... and they don't cost a thing. Although they all very much demand of us our hearts for the making; the making of a better world and life-experience, especially when psychological wounding has taken place.

I can speak most confidently on these things because I have found them to be so deeply true for my own healing and self-rediscovery journey. I have also found these things to be true through the experience of accompanying others on their own journeys, both in and out of my counselling practise.

We don't, and I believe can't, know everything, but perhaps what we know in our hearts to be true for us, from our own learning, growth, and experience, is *enough*. We come into an already made world, and we all one day will leave this imperfect ready-made world behind. No one truly knows where we were before we came, and whither we shall go and/or return, but I think we can relax and have faith. We can relax and have faith and still endeavour to put our best foot forward whilst in this world.

We can put our best foot forward and endeavour to create mini worlds that are overall good. And, for those of us who parent, we can give our young the best of possible starts, which by the way do not have to be perfect, *just good enough* – simply being more good than bad. And the same applies very much to the relationship we have with our own heart, our soul and our overall selves; the complexed human beings that we can be, who can love deeply, truly, profoundly, and can equally wound each other, deeply and profoundly.

We don't have all the answers yet, so we continue to Quest.

On Eyes Wide Open:
Wake Up!

I was watching a TV show and I was enjoying the programme until it came to the part of the person's story where he found out his relatives were slaves...

I can sometimes avoid these stories/topics because it is so upsetting as they are talking about my family tree too. One slave owner discussed on this programme, used to beat the pregnant women/so-called slaves so badly that they would give birth. They would also beat them so that the women would give birth sooner so these poor excuses for human beings could get the child and exchange him/her for a quicker buck!

Imagine that for a second.... that child's introduction to the world absolutely traumatised from the start; forced out because some greedy twisted monster, far from "master", has devalued human life to make money from it. How does a mother, a human being, recover and live with that heart and soul, mind-blowing, soul-destroying experience?!

These monsters also recorded slaves' deaths as *'decrease'* because slaves/human beings were solely seen as property.... *DECREASED earnings!*

Who are the sick, depraved and morally corrupt humans here?

Some of the 'owners' of these slaves/human lives lived not in the Caribbean. Mr Dutty (Jamaican slag word for dirty) Dallas lived in the Caribbean doing the *real slave owners' dirty work;* small time Dallas getting paid for his part, whilst Mr Real Slave Owner, for example, lived in London, Brunswick Square, receiving his BLOOD MONEY from the comfort of his 'well to do' armchair!

I know stories like these are true, and some are even worse still. I know this, because as part of my healing, becoming, and mis-education **RE**-learning Sankofar Journey, I had to take a trip down my ancestral memory lane. I had to do so to satisfactorily put to bed the racism I had internalised living in a world sharply divided by race and sex and mis-education.

Speaking of education, as a youth at 11 or 12 years old, as young as I was, I was flabbergasted that at school in History lessons when the subject of slavery was taught, it came under the heading of the 'Slave Trade.' And not only was it under that heading, but as part of the lesson, we were taught how economically viable the slave trade was - even for the slaves themselves! Especially *after* slavery! Think how psychologically and historically wounding to developing black-child's mind this is - and the white child. Feeding the white child the destructive and divisive white supremacy racism addiction, whilst giving the black mind a soul-destroying inferiority complex that we are 'no things' and as such we do not matter, loud and very clear for anyone awake and sensitive enough to hear.

Slavery, like any personal trauma, is insidious.

Its destructiveness, outright viciousness, immorality, pathology continues to sweep through the personal and the collective, across generations. The world and its inhabitants find it hard to reckon with this, but this uncomfortable truth does not become less true just because the world chose to look away and pretend its impact and continuing presence is no longer here today.

Everything that is happening and exists today, has its roots. Slavery/racism/white supremacy is rooted in destructiveness and is , and has been, *running a serious infection*. The infected roots of slavery and racism. Notwithstanding the infected root of sexism. The infected root of being *inhuman* is evident in the Western man's inhumanity to his darker hue sisters and brothers.

A wise soul once said about humankind,

The question is not when will we learn,
but when will we act on what we already
know.

My writing, my self-expression and my vocation as a counsellor, are all mediums I use to act on what I know to be true in the heart and soul of me. My truth needs no defence. It just *IS*... the same today as it was yesterday and shall be tomorrow.

I choose the light. That's where love resides. Love heals, love ousts fear, love makes all clear. Love is and does so much, but love don't play. Love demands the absolute best of us, in all our brokenness. Love wants our light. Haters be warned, she wants yours too. Conscious-up. Come out of the dark. Life is meant to be basically good. Do your healing, and for love's sake, be kind: human kind, like. And if that is hard, go get some bloody help and stop spreading your pathological hatred all over the place!

On The Pandemic of Black-on-Black Crime:

Inner City Blues... Make Me Wanna Holler

The following is a post I wrote on social media, which I have expanded on a bit further in this book following a recent spate of black-on-black knife and gun crime. At the time of writing this (07/04/2018) there has been 55 fatalities of such crimes - not forgetting the loved ones they leave behind as casualties of broken hearts and difficult grieving processes, especially with these deaths being primarily young black boys and young black man. Parents aren't meant to be burying their children in their youths before they have fully lived, let alone left school.

An Analogy:

So, say you have a disease, like cancer, and the doctor tries to heal it by giving you an operation on your arm... a place where there is absolutely no cancer. Or, the doctor tries to treat you by giving you lots of pain killers and sending you away, free of charge, on the most lovely of holidays. Would you recover from the cancer, a cancer that is already at a life-threatening stage? Would you heal? You will agree with me that for the cancer to stand a good fighting chance of being cured, the doctor would have to go to the root of the cancer and work on recovery from there.

THE SAME THING APPLIES TO THE INCREASE IN KNIFE CRIME AND GUN CRIME AND THE YOUTHS WHO ARE DYING, WAY BEFORE THEIR TIME.

Measures to resolve this ongoing crisis of young black males' extinction, needs to come from *all angles*. Work is also needed to clearly name and identify the root causes of this fast-becoming epidemic. Pandemic. This problem of neglecting to start from the root cause up, is a thing that is generally missing and extremely widespread in this very broken world.

Nothing ever goes away until it teaches us what we need to know. - Pema Chodron.

History repeats, both personally and collectively, across generations, and it spreads globally because we have not learned what we need to learn. To me, that should be the point of History lessons in schools - to *learn from the past mistakes of the previous generations*. When it comes to what the root causes are, much research has already been done and sits gathering dust from not being picked up enough and utilised, especially at the level of government and policy.

This world is crying out for change; for change in the old ways of seeing and dealing with real issues. This world is screaming out for a paradigm shift that overthrows the old order that never truly worked for every man, but just a privileged few.

The word Government has GOVERN in it, and as Daniel Goleman points out in his book 'Emotional Intelligence',

Leadership is not domination. It's the art of persuading people to work toward a common goal.

The word discipline comes from the word *disciple*, which means to *teach*... not solely to beat. So, going back to beating children and causing them to fear us as parents, is not the answer either. Indeed, many people who solely rely on this kind of discipline pedagogy, are very much part of the problem of inner city violence. Young people need firm and fair discipline, boundaries and displays of kindness; they need the adults in their charge to model the behaviour they expect the children to pick up. *Children learn mostly from what adults do, not from what they say.* Societies needs the same.

As people in charge and in governance of the young, we need to 'walk the talk'. We need to model to them what authentic leadership looks like. Expecting children to embody qualities that we ourselves lack as caregivers, teachers, politicians and the like, is absolutely ludicrous. It is like expecting a child, and/or an adult for that matter, to know how to do algebra without ever being taught... Madness.

Just had to put pen to page and shout out my way of looking at and understanding this pandemic of young people killing young people. As Malcolm X said,

No man truly understands until he wishes for his brother what he wishes for himself.

Young black men should not be dying before they have had a *fair shot* and a *chance* at shining their light. Parents and grandparents should not be burying their young like it's the *'done thing'*. Let's not normalise this! It needs to stop!

And *breathe...*

POEM: Transitions

New Old Soul
Passage
Dark Safe Warm

Joy Waters Life
Body
Breath Lights Time

Sweet Peace Serenity
Rampant
Emotions Waves Frustrations

Fearful Waiting Wanting
Conditions
Gratification Comforts Yearnings

Hope Plays Imagination

Trusting
Fun Loving Faith

Exploratory Independent Discovery
Self
Sexual Sensual Pleasures

Artistic Creative Expressions
Spirit
Intuition Whispers Voices

Instinctual Inner Learnings
Pure
True Wholesome Relations

Seasons Breeze Infinity
Free
Me Two We

One.

On Being Human:
Human Doings

Human-doings, that is what we have become. Twenty-four hours we are given in a day and we action it to the hilt. Mankind is truly making progress in becoming actual machine. The glorification of busy is at full speed. We treat ourselves and drag around our bodies like some dead weight, as if the body won't exact certain cause and effect payment. We do the same to the earth.

We are the only species in the world that work so hard at being anything *other than itself*. Apples aren't trying to be oranges; elephants, giraffes; pigs, foxes... We have allowed our minds to run amok and get stuffed with what the world says is good, and a good look, for us.

Maybe I find this easy to talk on and recognise because, since I was a child, I never wanted to follow anything or anybody. I wanted to be myself... well, once I gave up on wishing I was a long-haired little white girl. I wanted to set my own standard, watch the latest film, get this or that particular gadget or outfit, but when I got round to it not when everyone else was on the hype trip.

I seem to have been born with an inbuilt aversion to following popular opinion. If I am going to be a part of any crowd, it is the crowd of the underdog, the fringe-dwellers. Those who stand just enough on the outside of things, looking in, so as not to get lost in 'other' - a lack of presence and perspective that obscure the much bigger and more important picture.

I'm never with the 'popular' because I have already experienced and paid a high traumatic price for not fitting in, based on looks. I have already had front row seat to the 'normal;' to the 'popular;' to the 'that's the way of things, so why change it?' Change it because that way stinks! Because that way is unfair and cannot wholesomely prosper, being inhumane and unjust by its very nature. Soon the cause-and-effect chicken must come home to roost, and I don't want to be in the vicinity when all hell breaks loose.

So, the morale of this reflection is, just because most people do this or that, does not make this and that the thing to do - it just means that those people lack the foresight and courage to go against the tide and increase life. It just means most people find it hard to think for themselves, and use well, that warm blooded mammal brain we have been given. The brain which some have argued, supposedly, makes us far superior to the animals... hmm... questionable.

I do not buy into that at all. At least animals are being true to who they are and living their lives as their lives have been designed to be lived. They have that on lock down; we have our true self on lock down because we are afraid to be singled out; to stand alone. That is why I love love *love* people who go out on limbs, even if they don't have what is considered talent, they tried - so brave! In mine and the eyes of Life, *who dares wins*.

By my own daring nature, I have come to feel very comfortable holding my corner. I have come to feel quite at home standing alone, especially when I dare to take a stand and say what is in my heart and soul, going against the status quo. And when I am coming to the end of my time, whenever that may be, at least I would die knowing I was me, and I fulfilled who I was called here to be. That I didn't die with that wonderful music locked inside me; that I danced to my own humane tune!

That is the peace of mind I fall asleep with every night which, I believe, is a kind of dress rehearsal for the coming end of transient time. I have my priorities right and am daily rehearsing well. So, to my mind, when nature calls, having to endure the 'this too shall pass' discomforting fear of being my 'uncomfortable truth' self, is a very small price to pay. This sweet, surrendered peace of mind, no amount of money, mask or fitting in will ever be able to buy.

Although they do try, and the powers that don't know how to *be*, daily endeavour to milk us dry.

This way of being for me is my daily bread, as mankind in their right mind, cannot live happily and well by materials alone. And the top prize? I get to keep this peace and have it live, rest and abide in me... even when I am challenged by the various existential life-givens that comes with this very human condition!

Yes, this is the Life I *choose* every day to be living, remembering that I am not my life's contents: I am Life, Her very good self!

On The Forward Movement Of Life:

The Fear of Change

In the sequence of the creative process, every need or desire is first an idea before it is an object: the order of life is 'inner' before 'outer.'

This following piece was written December 31st, 1999, at the turn of a new millennium. It had felt like quite an historic event in the map of The Story called humankind.

A Time for Change

As we enter a new year and a new millennium, perhaps now would be as good a time as any to take inventory on our lives by asking ourselves the following key questions:

Who am I? Am I really who I say I am? Am I all I ought to be?

Maybe our New Year's resolutions would stand a much better chance of becoming actual realities if we took the time to address these questions openly and honestly.

The Need for Change; The Fear of Change

Change isn't always easy, however, it is a necessary and intrinsic part of life. Change is the natural movement in the flow of life. Everything changes, nothing remains the same. Life is change. To resist change is to go against the natural order of things, a way of living and being that creates all manner of internal and external conflicts, disease and disharmony.

If ever there was a need and a time for change, it is now. We are living in an era where many of the myths and misconceptions that have been an integral part of our lives and education, are now being exposed as blatant distortions of the truth. Mis-education and the denial of truth seem to be the order of the day and, as a result, in every area of human activity, there is conflict, imbalance, and unrest.

You may try and distance yourself from this state of affairs, however, it would be wise for you to remember this ancient African saying:

Whatever happens to the individual, happens to the whole group, and what-

ever happens to the whole group, happens to the individual.

We all need to take personal and collective responsibility over our lives and the world we live in.

A Change of Mind; A Change of Heart

Today you are totally different in every physiological sense than you were three, five, seven years ago. The question is, *how different is your mind?* Have you taken the time to change your mind, to heal your heart? Or are you still stuck in the past re-experiencing the same old experiences, emotions and worn-out habits? How free is your mind? Have you emancipated yourself from the chains of mental slavery?

The Mind is a Terrible Thing to Waste.

Imagine what kind of a world it would be if we all dared to change our minds and hearts about life. Imagine what kind of world order this new mindset would create. Go on, imagine it; don't be afraid to dream...

In the sequence of the creative process, every need or desire is first an idea before it is an object.

The Many Faces of Fear

Fear has one major and vital life function and that is to help us to survive when we are in danger (actual or perceived), to enable the body to mobilise itself swiftly and efficiently to protective action. Outside of this, when fear is more imagined than truly real, mostly played out in our minds, negatively affecting our physiology and well-being, it is then considered as a low life form fear. Fear, in this instance, then becomes a false expectation appearing real: an absence of trust and faith.

Fear is epidemic in our society. We fear so many things: being alone, making decisions, finding a new job, ageing, criticism, losing control, asserting ourselves, opening our mail... the list is inexhaustible. Long-term denial of fear puts us further and further out of touch with reality.

Prolonged fear over a long period of time creates all kinds of psychological disturbances, such as panic attacks, phobias, obsessions, compulsions, depression, agoraphobia, psychosis. Additionally, fear narrows our lives and our experience of the world, blind fear also underlies all inhumane acts of violence and organised genocide. It is wise to get a handle on fear.

Turning Fear into Courage

It takes emotional courage to change. You need courage to recognise enough of what's going on, to realise that change would be a good thing. So, tap yourself on the back for coming this far already, not just in terms of this article, but in life in general. I know that most of you have faced various trials and tribulations in your lives and have managed to come out on the other side - intact. I am sure that you can remember a time when you found the courage to change some aspect of your life that was causing you great pain and difficulty. To keep on keeping on in this world is not only an **act of faith**, but an achievement in and of itself. Never forget to recognise and celebrate your achievements.

Facing Our Fears

Did you know that our greatest problems in life come not so much from the situations we confront, but from our doubts about our ability to handle them? It then follows that *all we need to do to diminish our fears, is to develop more faith and trust in our ability to handle whatever life may bring.* The following guide is designed to help you further develop and strengthen the tools and insight needed to dismantle your fears, fly out of that cage, and realise your *in*nate potential:

- The next time you are in the grips of fear, be still and breathe. Don't waste time or energy running from your fears. Embrace fear, make it your ally. You cannot solve a problem without first staring it in the face. Get a grip on fear before it gets a total grip on you and your quality of life.

- Make a concerted effort to understand the underlying causes of anxiety and fear. This will help you to tackle the real problem, or the root cause. Then tell the truth to yourself; the truth will set you free, loosening that bit further fears' grip.
- Express yourself. Keep a journal, pray, meditate and cultivate trusting relationships with others to help you monitor, challenge, root out and transform negative thought patterns. Override them with the more life-affirming, soul-sustaining, nurturing ones.
- Set yourself a programme to tackle particular fears, one at a time. For example, if your fear is crowds, set yourself the goal of facing and speaking to more and more people every week. Do not set such high goals that are bound to fail, but be realistic; acknowledge and accept where you are, then move forward from that point on. Small, steady, certain steps, like a toddler persevering in her efforts to walk - falling seven times, getting up eight.
- Give yourself major credit for your efforts. Give yourself regular treats and rewards for the courage you are showing. Facing fears can be very scary, especially to begin with, so you are

doing a brave new thing... you are happening on the road less travelled.

- Learn relaxation techniques and practice them. While you are relaxing, imagine what you fear, and try to make peace with it. With relaxation, visualisation and meditation you can control fear. Relaxation is a major key in healing and success, so it too is worth persevering with if you find relaxing difficult. There too, start small.

- Seek help through your doctor, a qualified counsellor, or minister if you feel that the first steps are too difficult and you need further support. Realise that this does not make you an oddity, but human. It takes a lot of courage to reach out for help, especially if that too has been a difficult thing to do.

- And lastly, remember the wise words of Alice Walker when she said,

Every small positive change we make in ourselves and in our worlds, repays us in confidence in the future.

Beyond Fear

Educate a man and you educate an individual. Educate a woman and you educa-

tion a nation. - Dr James Emman Kwegyir-Aggrey

As a holistic counsellor, with over 13 years' experience in the counselling and personal development field, (in 2022, thirty-six years experience to date), my sole purpose and life's work is very much based on the ancient adage and wisdom of ***Know thyself.*** Time and time again, I have had the privilege to bear witness to the miracles and possibilities that such self-knowing can and does bring. I also speak from personal experience when I say, that once you have come to know, love and accept yourself for all and everything that you are, there is nothing you cannot achieve. This is the hardest and a more than worthy cause, not just for the individual and her world of relationships, but for the very earth and collective human relationships across the board (of once divide).

So, as we welcome in this new millennium, remember to be gentle and patient with yourself; love, support and nurture yourself throughout your (un) learning, becoming and healing... Feel the fear and continue to climb that mountain of inside-out freedom, anyway.

You can do it! You have the power and ability within you to handle all of life's situations. *Know thyself and to thine own self be true,* not some other made-up commercial version of you!!

Godspeed on your backwards, upwards and onwards journeys!

On Inspired Burning Desires:

My Reason For Being...

If something deep inside you is not happy
and has secret shadow desires, the thought
of which, when they arrive, satisfies
this ancient longing inside; then do That thing!
choose That thing! And live!!

My burning desires are writing, healing, and
    deeply relating,
whilst living my best life experience possible,
as identified and **RE**-defined by That deep
    restless
thing inside, who only finds The Sweetest Peace
    Of Mind

when I nurture, nourish, and give Her ample
    opportunities

toward True Self-Expression.

She is, the Soul I have been blessed with,
and have come here to embody and fulfil;

everything else falls behind - and stands in line
    before her -
of which I offer no apology...

POEM: A Just Cause

Enter me,
Cause me to go under and better stand
the getting to Know me.

Cause me

to find and heal those places inside
where time stood still, making me ill.
Enter me, Cause me
to become better acquainted
with the depths of my soul-
It's highs and it's low.

Cause me

to know what life's all about, then
lovingly let me die to the old,

and give breath to the New
life growing inside.

Cause there's no me without you,

so, enter and forever educate
and make me worthy of having you
Enter and Cause Me.

Part Three: She Who Must Be and Can Never Be Turned.

When the Soul wants to experience something, she throws out an image in front of her and then steps into it.

- Meister Eckhart

POEM: Sweet, but Street

She is a Child of Love;
a Sweet, but Street kind of Love,
that's Real Kind of Love.

Bathed in positivity, She Is,
because We Are, Her Beloved Children -
and Her Mission? To Preserve All Her
Be-Loved Like Creations.

The Breath and Depth of Her Love,
Informs the Heart of Her Craft
of Fleshing out the bones
of the Mind Body and Souls
of all Her Misguided Relations.

Her Truth and Right Justice IS,
exactly the same, and like Good Music,

when it hits you, you **Feel,**
no pain.

But don't get confused thinking
you can play Her Love for fool, for although
She's Sweet, She's also Street, and
Her Bittersweet Golden Rule?
Who don't Hear Must Feel.

So, treat Her right, She's your Queen,
and Her Love Reigns Supreme.
Now, take Her hands, and let Her take you to
You are most Precious,
Sweet Dreams...

On Missed Education:
Lady Sings The Blues

The Blues Ain't Nothing But The Sun Trying To Shine...

Feeling down, way down low,
not knowing where to turn,
or how to go.

Black and Blue - lonely too,
feeling like such a fool,
all grown, and never schooled
in matters of The Heart.

Longing to get high -
so high; to supply I and i
with the right wings I need to fly
and escape this alienated existence.

Hungering for attention,
a mirror, a Real Reflection -
in desperate need of affection;
a small dose will do -
just enough to see me through.

Oh! The absence of another's presence,
the history and pure agony of it
leaves an aching, a waiting, a wanting
in my soul, that refuses to be filled with just
anything.

It is time to be still, this I know,
a difficult pill to swallow,
when Love-starved Ego wants to Go! Go! Go!
and give into the temptation
to persist in self-abnegation.

Defiant, defensive,
terrified of caving in,
freezes out tender feelings,
a battle ensues within.

Energy drains;
feels like I'm going insane
as I surrender to ancient fears and pains,
realising that they too are me, dying
to be acknowledged, and set free.

Enlightened, Revelation Dawns
forbidding, foreboding clouds and storms;
reassuring vulnerabilities-
wizening out ambiguities, lets,

And Still I Rise!

Fresh Air In.

A New Day arrives,
as rainbow coloured tears cry,
clearing grey skies,
giving way to Golden Rays of Sunshine,
that throw my Soul Out,
before me-Self-ACTualised.

To this Present, Time
is where you find me
standing on the other side, Real Eyes In
That the Blues, **the Blues ain't nothing
But the Sun trying to Shine.**

So, maybe next time round,
when I am feeling upside down,
I will remember to Let Go, Let God & Pray -
and move my sweet behind
out of harm's way!

On Emotional INtelligence:
Heart of The Matter

Emotional Intelligence is the Difference That Makes the Difference. - Daniel Goleman

In the previous poem entitled *'The Blues ain't nothing but the Sun trying Shine'*, the subject matter is the world of emotion: a much needed and missing education. It was not until I went into therapy, that I began to get to know this world of emotion that bit better, as well as intimately. Before then, I had learned to stuff my emotions and dress them up in issues around food and, whenever needed, dump them in the dustbin of bulimia - the latter behaviour some time ago now.

In therapy I learned that emotions exist and that they go on existing even when unacknowledged and deeply buried. I also learned that emotions are legitimate and that

I was more than entitled to my own. I began to learn how to recognise and identify my feelings and emotions, distinguishing one from the other; befriending the ones that were most troubling to me, like fear, sadness, anger, *vulnerability*. All of which is very much a process and takes a good deal of time, as well as courage, to embrace and reconfigure. As one wise soul rightly said,

It takes more courage to be moved by emotion than it takes to deny pain.

It is very important to understand that emotional intelligence is not the opposite of intelligence, it is not the triumph of heart over head - it is the unique intersection of both. - David Caruso

In therapy, as I was getting a much-needed education in the world of feeling and emotion, I came to know how important this education is. This **RE**-learning first took root during the eating disorder therapy group I attended which, in 1987, kicked off my healing and self-discovery journey. During that bout of therapy, when my emotions began being attended to by the two very kind and compassionate psychotherapists facilitating the group, the need for an eating disorder began to make its way out. This was so significant because, the way I was with bulimia and food up to that point, I had seriously thought that I would never be able to shake myself free of it.

I had seriously feared that I would never be able to release the compulsion to binge-purge eat and use food in this unconsciously driven way whenever I was stressed in *any way* or when I was experiencing feelings I couldn't cope with. Bulimia, and my overall troubled relationship with food, was a way I attempted to emotionally self-regulate, a way that had turned into a coping mechanism for me. So, when the emotional intensity went out of bulimia, on that basis alone, I came to learn and know that the world of emotion is very important and should be given more attention. Not just at home, but in classrooms, and spaces and places where people come together to learn and promote personal growth. It was that relief and emotional release I experienced in therapy, that made me decide to become a therapist myself and pass this gift-baton of emotional freedom back onto others imprisoned in Loss: the loss of The Authentic Self and its true self-expression.

We define emotional intelligence as the subset of social intelligence that involves the ability to monitor one's own and other's feelings and emotions, to discriminate among them and to use this information to guide one's thinking and actions. - Salovey and Mayer

It is not enough to assume that this form of emotional **IN-**telligence will be automatically present in the homes of children, as oftentimes this missed education gets handed down across generations. People cannot give what they don't have; cannot teach what they have never learned. Some people can do this, those who are naturally more in touch with the Inner-world side of themselves and **IN-**tuitively have a natural way with emotions - which I am one of, however (once) maimed. When it came to caring for others and attending to their needs, I was Master of Ceremony. I gave from what I was not given, and had desperately hoped to have been given, intuitively knowing that it was important to my development, so would be great for other's development too.

Also, mixed in with this knowing, was the hope these others will learn from me, and in turn give that care back to me. This was the hope I held with regard to my own parents... my first/erroneous experience of what love is and how to give and not receive it.

If you are tuned out of your own emotions, you will be poor at reading them in other people. - Daniel Goleman.

Adults who were not attended to emotionally by their own caregivers, have not learned what they need to know to make positive contributions to their own children's world of emotion, keeping the emotional baton stuck in reactive inactivity. Most parents go on to do the best they can, whilst others look forward to turning the tables in the spirit of *hurt people hurt people*. And others still, albeit unconsciously, simply pass the baton unauthentically on. And then when shit eventually hits the fan (e.g. youth violence and overall disrespect of authority), society blames the young, much like a bad workman blame his tools for the poor state and performance of his work.

Whilst some parents, like myself, make the conscious decision to treat their children differently, vowing to break the destructive chain, they do so by actively living and implementing the revered golden rule of treating others how we would wish to be treated ourselves.

Some adults find it hard to imagine and grasp that, although they are children, children are equal to adults as fellow human beings; worthy of respect, good treatment and emotional nourishment. Some adults do not grasp this, even when their children grow into adults themselves. Even then they still want to apply that misguided 'personal-power-once-denied at the opportune time' hungry angry upper hand. As the quote below *RE*-Minds:

> *Leadership is not domination. It's the art of persuading people to work toward a Common Goal.* - Daniel Goleman

You may find such adults talking about 'these children' and how 'this generation have it easy'. You may find them viewing the world in terms of *'us'* and *'them'*, all of which

115

is very unfortunate and sad to me. These kinds of adults I find triggering to be around and, wherever I can, limit the time spent with them. Not that I solely take my children as friend. Some parents can swing in the opposite direction because of how unfairly they themselves were treated as children. I very much parent and take that role very seriously. However, and fundamentally, I see (my) children as equals and worthy of being given mutual value, respect, and attention. This I see as a 'given' that children do not need to earn. Children do not owe us for giving them life; it is us who give them life, that owes them the gift of those optimal conditions that make their life worth living, and worth paying that gift forward.

Truly I tell you, I believe and understood what Jesus meant when in the Christian Gospel it is said that He said:

Let the little children come to me, and do not hinder them, for the Kingdom of Heaven belongs to such as these.

For me, metaphorically, what was being presented and expanded upon here was an 'honour thy children.' After all, it has also been said that we can't get into the Kingdom without first coming to be as little children...

If your emotional abilities aren't in hand, if you don't have self-awareness, if you are not able to manage your

distressing emotions, if you can't have empathy and have effective relationships, then no matter how smart you are, you are not going to get very far. - Daniel Goleman

I believe that it is when we have been emotionally educated and have a good and sound emotional intelligence, that we become *truly human,* and, as a natural consequence, *humane.* This kind of intelligence cannot be brought or academically learned about in sterile clinical conditions. It is not just the child that has been abused, or has been generally un-nurtured, or is experiencing emotional absent caretakers because of financial hardships and all the stress and extra hours of work that can come with it; no, it is not just these groups of people that can go without this important socialisation - or humanisation if you like - but also the so-called highly educated and privileged.

Oftentimes, as children, the privileged run into (the trauma of) boarding schools - schools that have little time for this kind of emotional socialisation - and they are brought up in families and environments that puts much more stock in academia and having 'proper occupation'... often meaning nothing creative and nothing that places one's personal happiness as cornerstone. This way of thinking views education as being much more about 'being done to', of 'inputting' and 'programming' information, at the expense of self-expression, innovation, originality. An educational experience that lacks imagination and life becomes seen and experienced *literally*. How incredibly one-dimensional and uninspiring.

As John Bradshaw reminds us in his book, 'Home Coming-Reclaiming And Championing Your Inner Child':

Children are naturally predisposed to love and affection. However, the child must first be loved before he can love.

Ashley Montagu shares a similar view in his book 'Growing Young':

Of all humanising need; beyond all others it (love) makes us human.

It is never too late to take up this important humanisation process (I like that concept); you can teach yourself and experiment in relationships. You can also go into therapy. Therapy's main subject and focus is relationships and the world of emotion: re-igniting and enlivening that life force and spiritual life flow.

Counselling is not only for tackling 'problems', it is also about self-development and learning to re-engage the forward movement in one's life, especially after long periods of true life arrestment and stagnation. Counselling is also useful for realising dreams and developing the self-confidence 'to live the life imagined,' as Henri Thoreau wholeheartedly encouraged.

And above all else, counselling can help us to 'Know Thyself', as the Ancient Founding Mothers and Fathers advocated, being wise enough to recognise and know, through the learning from experience, that this is the knowledge, above all knowledge, that makes all the difference to the quality of one's life, humanity and the collective. This self-knowledge brings with it peace, love, and harmony, and is as true today as it was yesterday, and as it will be tomorrow. That is the way Universal Truth is and lives. When we do not know ourselves, we fail to recognise and put into full effect, our unique gifts and talents - the gift and talents humankind and it's manmade world needs to survive, thrive and optimise.

In the last decade or so, science has discovered a tremendous amount about the role emotions play in our lives. Researchers have found that even more than IQ, your emotional awareness, and abilities to handle feelings will determine our success and happiness in all walks of life, including family relationships. - John Gottman.

So, move especially out of literalism and originate. Go *generate and enrich* your Life, *find and release* your Flow, and *'liven-up yourself'*, as Bob Marley said. And to quote John Muir on the subject of Imagination..

The Power of Imagination makes us Infinite.

Go **RE**-Imagine. Go live your unique superhuman myth.

On Love Being Here, With And Within Us:
In The Midst

In the midst of *RE*-newing ongoing life focuses, which keeps me committed to the decision I made in 1986 to become all that I may be, my youngest son - the wash belly, as Jamaicans can call it - has just experienced a second psychosis episode breakdown. This has me, just about, keeping my head above emotional waters. This experience has me currently feeling so very close to being tipped over this unexpected edge. A true test.

Thrown (back) into the world of carer, at a time I had just embraced the empty nest and had been further coming into my own, since first coming to be a mother at the early age of eighteen years old, by all of one month. Yes, thrown back into the role of carer. Big time. A totally unknown world, one I have to swiftly get my head around, especially as my son is a young black man, and to help him through the mental health system, I *have to be* there with him every step of the way, throughout 'treatment.' No decision is to be made without my being there. Ain't no lie, at times it feels like the Universe really has it in for me...

This situation is truly testing my resolve and is asking of me to dig even further into what already feels like dwindling inner reserves. And in the midst of all this, the world just keeps on moving, regardless, and I continue to be Called from a Higher Source to continue to blossom on The Path that I am on, regardless - to not lose sight of that *Purposed Prize*. Feeling the magnanimous warmth of The Light from The Source, also sourced within me, keeps the twin flame of Hope and Faith alight in me and in my life... my life at this harrowing time. Some kind of journey.

I have had this life, this drive and this awareness inside since a child; one that keeps me carrying on and inclining to believe and cultivate greater faith in The Good that absolutely rules the world. I am to keep this in mind and hold it in heart, paying little attention to the myriad ways, every day, that life presents itself. In the face of this new challenge, that assurance is still, and always will, be there.

So, while a part of me wants to sink into despair and lament "Why me?!" (deserving its feet stomping moment), another side of me whispers, "USE EVERYTHING". Use everything life throws at me to sink more deeply into this inner knowing of The Good and True Essence of Real

Life, that moves from the **IN**-side. And outside, I am embraced by the true soul of the world.

Why not me? What makes me so special to be spared visitations from *difficult?*

And so, I roll up my spiritual sleeves and do what I am Called from Greater Heights to do, whilst taking the very best physical and psychological care of myself that is humanely possible. In the midst of it, I know that love is within me. As the One True Spirit of Love is with everybody, on our individual and collective Life Journeys.

On Turning To Love:
I Accept; I Surrender...

Surrender and Acceptance - my two Personal Powerhouse Assistants, that I am currently being called to make better use of.

Acceptance, Surrenders' little brother, is asking of me, for psychological well-being, to allow all that is currently on my plate to simply be there, for however long it needs to be. To take this time in my life one day at a time, and stretch that out further still when the going gets that bit more tough.

Troubles can come to feel like unwelcome visitors, over-staying their welcome and being totally indifferent to how incredibly challenged they can make you feel. And, sadly, I can inadvertently add to my suffering by trying to resist them by 'overthinking' mental gymnastics, in the hope of being rid of them.

But alas, we all have our crosses to bear on this earth-plane. As some wise soul once said, "The rain rains both on the just and the unjust alike." And as Existential philosophers and Buddhists have similarly said, there is suffering in the world - that's part of the deal of being in existence.

So, the most and least we can do is not add to our suffering, as doing so prolongs and keeps suffering coming, again and again and again. The most powerful, healing and peace-inducing thing we can do with trouble is to accept it, and as the 13th century Persian poet Rumi invites us to do in his poem 'The Guest House,' meet our troubles at the door laughing, letting them in. I am not quite at the meeting my troubles at the door 'laughing' stage, yet.

Oftentimes, hidden deep within our suffering, is a gem of divine wisdom, waiting to be received as the *joyous gift* it is. But, since we humans tend to like learning lessons the hard way, trouble has no choice but to keep come a-knocking, sometimes banging, at our resistant doors.

I used to think Acceptance was, and felt a lot like, defeat. Acceptance felt like giving in and choosing to be the loser. But it is not. *There is power in Acceptance.*

There is Power and Peace in Acceptance and, at the heart of it, simple sweet Surrender – Acceptance's big brother. In the act of Acceptance, the old unyielding me Surrenders to the authority of Love. And in that risk-taking vulnerability, my soul feels reprieved; free to truly live and love and fully be connected to that Inner Source that sustains the whole, and me.

The way to Surrender is through Acceptance. There is no other route. Also the act of Acceptance increases Trust, Faith and Patience in a process under its own *IN*-fluence.

And yes, in actual fact, Acceptance does feel like a defeat, and death even, albeit more psychological in kind. It is the letting go of socially sanctioned old and worn-out habits and prejudices, dying... hard. In Surrender we are saying, "I'm here, take me, as I am, and ought to be; take me in naked transparency. I commend my spirit to You. In You, and You in me, I am strong, incredulously even when I am weak. In your true self Love, I have my being."

So, don't get it twisted, *Surrendering to love* is a great act of courage and inner strength. Standing up, and falling down, for Love means following Her 'true and just' ways, righteously balancing out the scales. And as another wise soul once said, which also applies on the personal plane,

The further a society drifts from the truth, the more it will hate those that speak it...

Crucifying and assassinating the truth-tellers, then when they are dead and out of the way, giving them honour and praise. Death, be it physical or psychological, is oftentimes the price that gets paid for living a life that is wholeheartedly right for you. That is why some people do run scared, rather than stand still and face their fears...

Therefore, Surrendering to Love and following Love's ways, I say once again, is an act of courage and strength. It is also humbling and fills one with Grace.

Try Acceptance. Next time something not very pleasing happens to you, don't fight it - let it be, and let be the associated '*difficult*' feelings that comes with it. Start small and bear witness to the Peace and Emotional Release that flows from *bearing* 'the difficult' in this more radical self-compassionate and self-accepting way.

I have been using the rush hour on the underground to further strengthen this practise of Acceptance. Practise makes Perfect. Practise makes good-enough humans who, for the most part, strive to treat others right and as they wish to be treated. Yes, that ancient old golden rule, which from kindergarten we should have already been schooled.

I don't allow myself to get caught up (i.e. become unconscious) in the dense energy of competitiveness, fighting, pushing, shoving to get on the tube/to get on in Life; to get a seat, and basically have things go, *always*, the way that we want. I also practise releasing the temptation to move at that 'Armageddon coming' rat race pace. If someone pushes in front of me, I let them be.

At first, the egotistical side of me did not find doing any of this practise enjoyable, but the peace that comes with not allowing oneself to get caught up in fleeting unpleasant forgettable moments, is undeniable. And at the end of each day, I am that little bit less stressed because I have not given as much of my *Life Energy,* unnecessarily, away.

Oftentimes, what serves me as a good reminder on this journey is in that moment when the temptation to engage in power struggles beckons, I ask myself, "Is this random situation worth my Inner Peace? Is it worth me, through the daily build-up of stress, becoming dis-eased and unwell?" And for me, for the most part, the reply is a resounding "Hell No!"

It is all still very much a work in process but, like I said, the growing and lasting inside-out peace and joy, is more than worth it.

On Being With Time:
Time And I

From the beginning of *my* time, Time and I have had a difficult relationship. For a little while, Time was fine, but then it became more like the enemy - something needing escaping; something needing made sweeter of. Time felt lonely and long back then.

Then, when I came to a certain turning point in my life, Time felt like something I could, perhaps, get to know, and use to right wrongs.

Since then, my relationship with Time has been evolving. Now I can, more often than not, enjoy Time, no longer seeing it as the enemy as much. Now, Time feels more precious; I don't wish to rush, but savour, every delicious tick-tock of it. I wish to develop a more intimate relationship with Time. I want to learn, all the more, how to enjoy and appreciate it, not worrying about it running out or wasting it.

Now I feel like I can afford to get lost in time-space and let Time lift and hold me up. Now it feels like Time can, and is, working for me, and I, it. And never again will I use such words as "killing time". I just want to be at one with Time, and trust in Time, and work with Time; and overall enjoy *my* time here... being more consciously alive and aware.

And, what I do with and how I spend my time, is nobody's business but mine. Naturally, I extend the same courtesy.

On Being Here And Now:
The Eternal Time of Now

When I reflect on this *Eternal Moment of Now,* it gives me this feeling of reverence; of a bigger picture that I cannot get my head around, and that I am not supposed to. Which human being can get its head around Eternity? In all its glory? No physical body.

The Eternal Moment of Now fills me with a mystery; a mystery that includes me and is wonderful. What does it do for you?

It fills me with such Peace that maybe, just maybe, *IN* this world – one that appears mostly negative, with its great and daily injustices and mean spiritedness of a seemingly privileged few who believe they have the right to act toward other people with such inhumane disdain and callousness - some *(Great)* BEING has got this mess of a world. That, maybe, behind some reverent curtain, there is a Grand Design that we are being given hints of and that is getting lost in all the negativity this world likes to breed and feed on, keeping us blind. What are the hints of this Grandness we overlook and have mostly taken for granted, you may ask...

Just for a moment, think about how this body we inhabit wonderfully works; every molecule and atom, every part and sub-part joined *together* in this beautiful dance of keeping us all together; alive, kicking, well. Avoiding pain. Creating survival mechanisms, in case shit gets insane, at any age. Intricacy and complexity working together, without our interference and bidding, in perfect harmony. Imagine this great big universe of stars and planets and solar systems, all working together harmoniously, without us having a thing to do with it (thank goodness!) Divine *Inner* intelligence created this with*in*, creating the possibility, by the same token, that this can be made without too. As within, so without.

We as human beings are truly egocentric, believing we have control and dominance over a world we know very little about. A body and world that works beautifully, timely, magnificently and consistently; highly Creative by itself...

Destructiveness comes solely and mostly from our end.

The Eternal Moment of Now, the thought of it soothes my Soul and grounds my physicality in this earthly body; enabling me to feel some iota of safety and peace in a world so lost to itself, and so terribly caught up in projected self-hate. Rumi captured this Eternal Moment notion so well when he said,

You are not a drop in the ocean, You are the entire ocean, in a drop.

Which brings to mind another quote that speaks volumes to me in my entireties. That speaks to the Personal Collective of me, here on the earth plane, as an African/Caribbean Black Woman,

Sometimes a fruit falls from a tree and rolls so far away from its roots that it's no longer of the tree. The hard fall, and long journey, bruises the fruit so much that it totally changes it. It's the same way for some of our people. This is why some can't be awakened regardless of how much truth you present to them. This journey has totally brainwashed them to such a degree that they're no longer of the original tree. - Malcolm X

The Tree of Life; the time of Now. Who the cap fits, let them wear it. And if you don't like the fit, change it. **RE**-arrange it. Do something brave, new and different with it.

On Living One's True Shape, Form And Aim:
The Hero Is Me

My Hero is me. For the past 12 months I keep coming back to this conclusion, especially when I am making certain strides and while I am keeping my *well-being goals*. Some of these goals are keeping to my meditation practice this past 5 years, others are keeping to my 3 times a week jog in the park, come rain, snow, or shine; being more Present in my relationships and putting myself in a position to have my needs met in them. I am also proud of myself for feeling the fear and stepping up at work anyway, and I am very proud of myself for putting myself through the training and volunteer work needed to work in the field that I love and make a good salary doing so. More recently, I am proud of myself for supporting my son who is going and growing through two episodes of psychosis, and of being able to resist the initial despair of having that situation on my plate, and proud of myself for not allowing the situation to turn me back around. Some kind of journey!

Proud of my kind and caring heart that cares for so many others, making a qualitative difference in their life journeys. I am happy to accompany them all in a purposeful way coming very much from the old adage that people *come into our lives for a reason, a season and/or a lifetime.* Our job is to figure out which one, take the necessary actions, learn the well intention lessons, and keep flow moving. And the icing on the cake? I then become one of the first people they then share with The Joy that overcomes pain, that lives well with the sunshine and the rain, the likes of which Frankie Beverly spoke about in his album 'Joy and Pain'. And as Rumi said,

Even the darkest night will end and the sun will rise.

I love that my life is filled with, and enriched by, this changing tide and its unchanging rhythm called life! It makes my experience of life ever so body-mind-spirit nutritious.

I do amaze myself, because walking on less-travelled roads is not for the fainthearted, hence the need for therapeutic accompaniment for those embarking upon it. I must say, our One True Spirit is pretty amazing.

Then there is this generosity of heart which I am blessed with; which has run into, more times than I had cared for, being taken advantage of. But going back to that wise adage about people, in those (key) relationships, I was still very much learning the reason and the lesson those situations brought to me, to reveal me, truly. This generosity of heart, however hurt in the past, I never closed the door on, as I truly love to love and doing so is free and freeing. You can't buy love. Love beckons,

"Come, no pretences. Come naked. Allowing vulnerability, and your deepest reaches."

When one comes like that, Love, in all ways **RE**-wards. Try it! It is this Love, this god or goddess, that has brought me to where I am today; to where, as a young girl, I knew I could be and reach, once I had adult jurisdiction afforded me.

Yes, I have come a very long way indeed and really don't take enough time to *recognise*, let alone to celebrate that fact. For me, this is what going to church has been made for - to recognise, reveal and celebrate our true selves and go out and share the good news that we have been awesomely made and have power for good in this world. In the down-to-earth unassuming church I attend, me, Life, Love, God, take that time to have a right old celebratory rave-up, having been made in our true nature, Perfect.

That's why I go to church. I do not go to church as 'sinner'. It is a sin and a shame this preoccupation with sin and shaming gets in the way of people coming to church... Perhaps the subject for another book!

Since I made the decision 31 years ago to prioritise me, my mental well-being, goals and dreams, I have remained steadfast despite the knocks, the bumps and the stalls along the road of coming back home to me as I am made to be. I am, we are, extra-ordinary. I am not coming at this self-appreciation from an egotistical self-absorption - far from it. I can still struggle with being noticed and feeling worthy of good things, a mental state born out of adverse childhood experiences. I am just taking the time to recognise, appreciate, celebrate, honour and enjoy the spirit that is me and bask in its testimony for this moment of time.

Another thing I love about me, is my silent power encased around an unassuming sensitive nature. I've grown into owning and appreciating that. I did not like it before because it seemed to make me an easy target for others, others unconscious of their true natures. On this journey I have reclaimed vulnerability, sensitivity, and diffidence. I *claim it* and oftentimes need to **RE**-claim it, over and over, because of that early mis-shaping and worldwide endangered species living humans keep choosing. As I get back and remain in One True Spirit shape, I accept this life I live and carve out for myself as artwork. As M.C. Richards said,

All the arts we practice are apprentice-ship. The big art is our life.

My life is my heArt.

What I love about me, is that even though my childhood was far from ideal, I did not allow it and I will not allow it, to have the final word on me; just like I did not allow my adversaries to have total influence and power over my development. Tenacity. I love that about myself. I love how that side of me fought tirelessly, keeping me as safe as safe could be, until I had more reign over what happens to me. And from thereon, from 18 years old, I have not let myself down. My hero!

I so now love this divine self-dichotomy I embody. One of fighting spirit, mixed with vulnerability, held together in self-knowing love. I love looking back at the stories of my life journey and of those various contemptuous unhealed others who tried desperately hard to test me. I, in turn, had to respond to The Call to have them meet my tenacious 'little friend', which they never liked meeting and saying hello to. They never liked having a taste of their own medicine, though taste it they should, to learn their own life lessons.

Another thing I love about me, and I am so grateful for, is my sense of Awareness; one that have never left me, and has been with me from the time I came out of the womb. I cannot remember a time that I was ever without it. This ability to see a bigger picture and see what is the matter; an innate seeing and knowing of right and wrong, and a dislike of injustice that never fails me. This quiet and observant knowing inside of me, always able to clearly see behind - behind behaviours, behind illusion and fabrications, understanding motives, both good and disastrous.

This innate (self)awareness that is so deeply a part of me, I love love *love*. It keeps me safe and out of harm's way, even when I am in the thick of it. It makes me stay true to my nature and it has a highly functioning conscience which I have had to learn to soften over the years as part of my healing, because it could have a hard edge to it.

I love self-awareness, even when I have to face painful truths; I cherish that innate and intuitive knowing so much. It keeps me straight, which means I can no longer stray from who I truly am. It also means that I can't take my shit out on others - not without feeling guilty and having to, wherever possible, say sorry afterwards. Being and living this way is also important to me because I love peace and the peace of mind that living authentically well brings with it. Yes, I love my peaceful nature and the sweet Surrender to the ways and things that affords my spirit *Equanimity*.

I could go on counting the ways I am delighted with myself and why that makes me my hero, but I think that is mostly it. I hope anyone reading this can find the hero inside themselves too, and similarly align to it, creating your Superhero Personal Collective Myth. It will bring with it battles, but **_The Joy_**... the joy far outweighs and outlasts the battle's painful aspects, making our efforts more than worth it!

You are - and we are - *more than worth it!*

On The Needs And Wants of Black Women Folk:

What Black Women Want

The most disrespected person in America is the black woman. The most unprotected person in America is the black woman. The most neglected person in America is the black woman. - Malcolm X

What Does A Black African American Caribbean British Women Want?

From the world, what she wants is to be equally valued, respected and treated just as fairly, as She is ancient and original Great Mother: all humans came from Her and return to Her. Although the world steals from Her, carbon copies Her, without credit; without shame. Like slavery days, when it was okay to beat Her, vilify Her, AND allow

145

Her to feed your child from Her breast... which tells me, deep down, you know Her true worth... as the following quote says,

The soul has no secret that the behaviour does not reveal. - Lao Tzu

Deep in your soul, you know; deep in the world's soul, it knows... *You can't keep a Good Woman down.*

From Her White Sistreens, especially in the world of work, what the Black Woman wants from you is for you to stop taking Her assertiveness and Her *fight against injustice,* so personally!

When She is targeted and gets caught up in it, in the isms and kisms, *stop calling that aggressive!* Own the aggression that the hand of privilege has raised you up on, then come again, corrected; then, maybe, we can become more united and together truly work towards the dismantlement of women-hating patriarchy.

And from the Brothers, don't get it twisted, before all this came to be, We existed, as One, in a Garden called Bliss, made in Love's Image; joined together in a Foundation of Ancient Civilisation. Founding Mothers and Fathers, as it was in the beginning, so shall it too be in the end...

So, embrace Her, don't chase Her away; she is your complimentary and *needs you in all kinds of ways*, as your struggle mirrors hers and is one of the same. If you hate on Her and deliberately choose as your pride *Other* than Her, know that (unconsciously) you are throwing shade and hating on yourself and on your race.

Choose another if you wish, just don't solely base that decision on wanting to get away with shit by playing 'guilt trip' and placing the Other on it. If there is hurt and rage at black women folks, heal thyself! I will leave it there. As Bob Marley said, "If the cap fits, wear it" - if it doesn't, there will be no need for defensiveness.

And to Us Sisters, please feel that you are allowed to lay down your arms, at necessary times, and do away with completely living out the myth of *the strong black woman.* That you most definitely are, but you are also very human. So, stop acting as if you can do it all by yourself and don't need no one else, least of all a man. That talk is just hurt and disappointment. Allow yourself to be vulnerable and, I promise you, all hell won't break loose. I know being vulnerable is difficult to do in a world where you are being constantly assaulted, overlooked, and abused, but for wellbeing's sake, you *simply must.* You're tired. Tired makes us miserable. Exhaustion makes us sick.

And with regard to being parents, let us all the more raise our boys to be grown men. In our love for him and how mistreated He too is in this world, we can sometimes unconsciously overcompensate, getting in the way of His growth, treating Him as an eternal little boy. And as young men and grown men, when they fall or the world knocks them down, don't rush to go pick them up; help them to rise up themselves. Give them the measuring stick of a King. Help them to experience the prophecy of true self-fulfilment.

And for the Girl Child, don't weigh her down so early in life with caregiving responsibility; let her have that room to breathe, to be, to please herself. Teach her self-care by modelling that behaviour yourself... that's how children learn, *not by what you say and don't do.* And, equally as important, teach her how to make and keep boundaries. By doing so you will save her from many a broken heart later on in life and keep her safe from perverts who prowl around childhoods, especially those without involved mothers and fathers.

As the following quote says about the value of boundaries,

Boundaries are the distance at which I can love you and me simultaneously.

I will leave the topic of hair, here (smiles).

This subject of *What Black Women Wants* is obviously very emotive for me as a Black Woman of African Caribbean Heritage; as a voice still unheard and unreck-oned with across the diasporas; relegated to the bottom of many a pile. But I smile because, you see, given a choice, I would still come back into this world as me, as there is a certain wisdom that comes from being in that bottom of the pile position...

I do not claim to speak for all Black Women. I speak from *my* experience of being one. And I speak from all the Black Women who have peopled my world, past and present. I write this piece to provide some clarity to those truly interested in knowing *What Black Women Wants.* This question has already been mused generically, based primarily on White European Women wants and needs, but, as you can see, as sisters, the world has made our needs and wants very different.

I have also created this piece as a tribute - a tribute I believe Black women are incredibly worthy and deserving of. So, when inspiration struck this week during my morning jog, I quickly had to put pen to page and overarchingly say...

You.
You Black Woman Are Beautiful, Original, Phenomenal...
You, We, deserve to be here! Here and equally cherished, protected, loved, revered!
You have been **Instrumental** in the making of this world!!

Life Sees You and Knows **Your Intrinsic Value and Worth.** I say that again,
Life Sees You and Knows Your Intrinsic Value and Worth.
My Sister, Mother of all mothers,
I SALUTE YOU!!!

On Fathering - Wanted And Needed:

An Appeal To Fathers

Oftentimes, and in the old days, Fathers were relegated to the side-lines of Family Life; to the background of things, with the world not fully grasping that your input is equally needed and valued.

Only you can protect in that super-powered way: the one that keeps predators away, keeping children safe.

I wish you can see how much children need you and how children can suffer so without your Presence and involvement. This I say to *all* fathers who father.

To the Black Fathers, specifically from African-Caribbean descent, my heart bleeds for you. It mostly bleeds because, in the Western world, your Power has been trampled on and taken away.

Your influence, ripped out from under you, especially when we were slaves. Its impacts still very visible and prevalent today.

There is nothing more I want to see, than the brothers standing tall in this society, **RE**-claiming and cherishing his family, taking back up that reverence residency.

Please, my brothers, come back home; our young'uns miss and need you so. They need that baritone voice that lets us, and the world know, exactly where the lines are drawn... to help us love ourselves, and our reflections.

Just like slavery, crack/cocaine came in the 80s to destroy the souls of black folks; no one pays/paid attention to that; no one does the maths. In the Americas it came, then to Britain, and the Caribbean.

But this Black Woman, this Sistah, this mother of sons, and aunt of daughters, loves you so, and to those of you gone AWOL, *come back home*... back home and seated in place of re/generation, enthroned.

Children are naturally forgiving. They just want their parents to see them, love them, teach them, spend time with them, keep them in line, give them that self-love and self-confidence they need in this life, to avoid being twice defeated in the race. Please believe, IT'S NEVER TO LATE.

It's never too late, if you've lost touch with your children, to put in the work. And if your children won't let you correct your mistakes, because it's taking them a minute or two to forgive your lack of previous involvement, there are many other unfathered boys and girls in need of your kind of time, your kind of care, your kind of protection, **IN**-fluence and love.

We need the black mother and father, together again. **RE**-united and loving up on each other, visibly, so our children can internalise how black love looks, loves, feels, acts. Brothers and Sistahs let's stop tearing each other up!

Too much inner-city trauma and blues. Now is the time to choose... to choose what's best for the children.

So, Daddies, come back home to the fold and let us, the black family unit, pick up where slavery plucked us from and our true stories left off...

Pick up and put ourselves back on The Map of Founding Mothers and Fathers, as Nature, not us, planned it.

Prodigal Father, come back home, the young'uns need you so!

Love and much Light.

Your Woman. Your one of a kind.

POEM: Dear Shadow
of Mine

Dear Shadow of mine,

Nobody has known of your façade aside from me,
not until recently at least. The chinks in your
    armour look so
accustomed to. So much so that you've forgotten
    who you
are. So much so that you've forgotten you're
    wearing
armour, and grew accustomed to a need to defend
your heart.

Dear Shadow of mine, your light shines bright,
    brighter
than you ever could believe. Just look at those
around you who yearn for your strength, the
    chinks in your

armour have only been showing your true colours.

I understand you're afraid of being yourself, you
    put the
armour on before you could remember, and this
    love that
you deserve may seem overwhelming, but it's all
    the love
in the world that you deserve.

You know this love all too well, with the smile of
    an angel
and the eyes of God herself. Born and cradled
    by the
vessel that could overcome, given nourishment
    by the
mind that could overpower and the heart that
    could
somehow over love.

My dear Shadow, you're so much more
than just yourself, you are light, you are love.
Fact of the matter is, your armour deserves rest, it's
    been over-
worn and over-distressed.

This light of yours deserves to shine,
around the world and across realities multiple
    times.

Embrace the love you've been blessed with and
    protect it
with all your heart.

Dear Shadow of mine, can you finally see, that
    you have
Been Light from the start.

This poem was written my beautiful son, Jamal James, who himself has the smile of an angel, the eyes of God herself, as well as an unlimited supply of reparative comforting hugs that he has generously metered out to me, his mother, over his 26 years. I don't remember real hugs from any adults during my 18 years as a child.

He wrote this poem just before his first episode of psychosis. He is now on the slow but sure *good news road of true self-**RE**-discovery.* His mental health crisis was triggered by the (untimely) death of his estranged father, whom he intended to seek out directly after completing university. The breakdown was brought on by the added stress of learning of his father's death in the final term of his final year at university, and smoking (too much) skunk weed to cope with it all.

So, any estranged fathers, and mothers, reading this here, it is never too late to reconnect with your children and help them (and you) emotionally and psychologically repair.

Today. Not tomorrow. Tomorrow is not promised, to anyone.

Part Four: Full Cycle

The path isn't a straight line; it's a spiral. You continually come back to things you thought you understand and see deeper truths.

- Unknown

POEM: All For One

I have two sisters, besides me -
All together we are three;
One's called Yesterday,
The other, Destiny.

We are forever here,
Occupying the same
Time, Space, Air.

My name's Precious, Gift
Because I am Present,
Without which, neither of us
Could be truly Present.

And when we are all living life as One,
Life feels like a breeze,
Like it's just begun.

But to be at one
With Destiny's plan,
Yesterday must be constantly undone.

So united we stand -
All For One and One For All,
Wholehearted **IN**-formants of
The Great I Am.

RE-membering ourselves
'til our work is done.

On Our First Society:
No Arms House

In the absence of the shoulders
of fathers and the arms of mothers, sisters and
    brothers,
let us still dare to live; to give expression to
the love once denied, and still awaiting
acknowledgment inside, if only that it may
by the same token - return to us tenfold,
and like a blanket help keep us warm,
bringing us back in out of the cold,
into the No Harms House that is a Home,
Sweet Home...

A place where Joy resides, and life includes
all things, rest assured it IS in the absolute
    knowledge
that we have always been *The Love we seek* -

Apple of the Most High, who sings The Tender
    Lullaby,
and remains forever at and by our side, for all our
    lives.

Safe Homes without harm,
Foundations with sturdy Paths...
Paths that have Heart and Spill Out
into the **out**-side of society.
As with *in*, so with *out*...

On Looking Back To Move Forward:

Back To The Future

You are what your deep driving desire is. As your desire is, so is your will. As your will is, so is your deed. As your deed is, so is your destiny. - Brihadaranyaka Upanishad

I have been revisiting James Hillman's works. His ideas truly resonate with my own and, in that sense, he *feels like* my soul brother. Since childhood, books and their authors have been like good family to me. Whilst listening online to his lecture entitled "Fathering the Boy Inside," Hillman asserts that therapy should not be solely concerned with the client's past; he believes this viewpoint to be quite limiting. He also shares that, while he is clear and decided on that, it has been an ongoing challenge to not fall under this limiting spell, having been well trained as a therapist within the psychoanalytic viewpoint of looking back on the past to solely identify root adverse behavioural problems and relational difficulties.

Hillman argues that more can be achieved, made whole and complete, if time, energy and theorising is spent, equally, looking to what Calls us to the future; to our personal and collective future, respectively; to our secretly held dreams of what we would truly like to be and do when grown. To identify those early experience of Callings, abandoned and overlooked.

To look back at the past, not just to discover the original wounds of what ails us in our 'now' situations, but to look back at experiences in the past (historic and otherwise) where we felt most inspired and alive. These moments and experiences hold the key to unlock once sealed off potential, that can help us discover our individual reasons for being, here, which must fall outside the so-called good opinions of others, which includes our parents, and the world around us.

He also argues and discusses this point of view in his book 'We've Had A Hundred Years Of Psychotherapy And The World's Getting Worse.' Yes, after a hundred years of psychotherapy, and yet conditions like depression and anxiety are at an all-time high, cutting across all sections of society.

He uses the analogy of an *acorn seed,* already containing within the unseen depths of itself, the oak tree; similarly, he believes that both personally and collectively, humankind can house within the very depths of its being, our future full-blown potential: the ALL of what we might be and come. All we need is the *optimal conditions to bring that possibility forth,* making it reality.

I am absolutely on the same page as Hillman, having given birth to my future self: to the self and the life that, as a young child, I felt compelled to imagine and one day experience. This was a vision and mission, if you like, that kept me *spiritually and psychologically alive* during very difficult and life-changing times. For the past three decades, since deciding on this '*self-healing, best life-realising*' journey, my self-***RE***-discovery went hand-in-hand with my heeding The Call, during my first personal experience of counselling, to become a Psychotherapist myself and share in making a similar *reparative difference* in other people's present and future lives.

The personal, as well as preservation of an *Alive Inner Life,* is political, especially when an ill- conceived worldview conspires to, and continues to, overlook this. It is more concerned with all things materialistic, capitalistic, and commercial. An ill-conceived worldview that puts a much lower price on human life than it does on actions that threaten its monetary investments. Let the evidence speak for itself: look at the prison terms served by rapists, paedophiles, domestic violence perpetrators and the like - that's if such cases even get to court and justice gets served. Crimes that destroy Inner personal lives; that cut deep across generations and take great efforts to recover well-enough from... these crimes against the person, more often than not, get no due recognition.

Not to mention the backlash that also comes back to bite us, the world and the society in the butt by what seems like a senseless and easy taking of human life; the kind that grabs attention daily in the papers and on the (nothing new) News... Which also hurts the economy by the big bucks it then takes to plaster over and throw peanuts at the problem, without truly looking at the underlying causes.

The Personal is Political...

Within my life and Counselling Practice, yes, space and time is given to the past and the task of dismantling, sufficiently, ingrained ill-conceived patterns and ideas about Self. And equally, time and space is given to identifying *patterns of possibilities* in need of more *life-affirming energising*. Ample time is given helping and supporting the client to move more confidently toward their most Compelling Life Vision, however dimly lit that vision is. A vision embedded within the genealogy of their Past Future Presenting Life. A vision that calls and cheers us on, secretly knowing the sweet fruits of its labour, laying in wait for the taking and realisation.

Not everyone working in the field of psychotherapy is working in this "*deeply enriching, difference-making, trans-*

formational" way; not everyone in the counselling field works at this relational depth. Not all – client and therapist alike, are able or willing, to act as midwife to future lives and dreams - rolling up one's sleeves and carry out the work of delivery, a works that takes blood, sweat, shit and tears. No less.

Not all are living and working at the service of creating Personal and Collective Wholeness. Not all are looking into the dreams, desires and aspirations that touch one's soul in the ways of Profound. There's still this "holding to" the skirt tails of being all 'separate' and 'individual', preferring that things happen toward its own means and ends (e.g. Brexit), without due consideration of the reality and importance of *Interdependence* and the everybody wins Prosperous Spirit of Cooperation. Hence, a hundred years of psychotherapy and little deep and lasting paradigm shift and change...

We are Life's work, Life's fruits, plucked from Her Tree. We hang on her Tree, along with Her other off spring: animals, minerals, stars, moons, planets. All these divisions, hierarchies and separatist ideas created arbitrarily in the "man-made" world, do not serve us or real life well. They do not serve **RE**-ality at all! Just ego.

Most of what we view as reality in this world, is brokenness. It is more of a living hell than anything else, particularly so for some of us. But not even hell can turn around what is to come and must have what it needs and wants.

Like the acorn seed and its deeply embedded oak tree, what is to come is already (secretly) secured, as well as absolutely guaranteed.

The reality we have been conditioned to believe we have to "get back to", embedded in the term *come back to reality*, is not Real. Only *Real* Is Real. Done deal!

So, when inspiration from the future calls "Jump!", I simply ask, "How high?" And I sow, I craft, I scribe and share from a more Joyful, more whole **RE**-alised self, and then Dreams come through into true being and space. For what are dreams? Dreams are what we call things that should already *be* and be how we live if we were less asleep and more awake, if we were less unconscious and had more **IN**-sight...

Fore,
I Am - We are -
Breathe of Life,
By Grand -
and Unfathomable -
Design.
With an Inner River
that holds the Potent Seed of
The Whole and All
that life, full of life, may Truly Be.
Seek out The Fringe Dweller;
Love and manifest what They Feel
See, Observe and *IN*-tuit.
Then go with
IN, and *RE*-lease The Dam
Of All that we may
All Become.

On Life Outside The Norm:
Fringe Dweller

I first heard the term **Fringe-Dweller** decades ago whilst reading Stuart Wilde's book, 'The Infinite Self, 33 Steps to Reclaiming Your Inner Power'. I most definitely identify as a Fringe-Dweller and have come across very many Fringe-Dwellers in my Psychotherapy Practice. A fringe-dweller feels ahead of their time, standing on the outskirts, and from that unique position *sees more* than the average folk. A position that makes life's road as a Fringe-Dweller, a lonely one. Feeling and being without a Pack, and that important sense of Belonging, can have Fringe-Dwellers feeling like something is wrong with them. That, in comparison to 'the normal' and 'the norm', they are abnormal based on the felt experience of being unlike your average folk. But we are not alone, and we belong, to Life, to Love.

For Fringe-Dwellers lost and without mirrors that truly see them and their unique Life Position, it's hard to truly see themselves and know their worth. *I see you!* This Inner Life Writes body of work is especially written for the likes of you!

So, stop straining to fit in and to be and feel acceptance therein. You will be Called soon - if you haven't been already - to share Your Light: to share what you see from that courageous stand-alone position. You emotionally brave human being. The time for The Voice Manifesting Sounds and *IN*-sights of the likes of you and I, is fast approaching. Ready your self-confidence.

New paradigms never get well-built by folks with poor I-sight, that lacks *IN*-sight. Just because most people do this and that, does not mean this and that is the way to go, let alone live. Fringe-Dweller, true life lives and longs for the likes of you. You better Believe. You better *Be and Live.*

On Living With Fear:
There Is No-Thing To Fear

Nothing real can be threatened; nothing unreal exits. Therein lies the peace of God. - A Course In Miracles

Quite a few years ago, when I first came upon the above quote, I was filled with such Peace; the quote truly resonated with me, right through to my core. Then, a short time afterwards, I had this dream. In the dream I found myself in a very scary situation. I found myself high up on a cliff, or a tower, and observed myself becoming instantly gripped by the fear that I might fall. In so-called 'real time', I have a fear of heights. Anyway, in the dream, as soon as fear gripped me, the above quote came to mind and fear left me. I looked down from where I was standing, into the abyss below, and thought to myself, "Even if I was to fall, I would feel nothing because the only real thing here is me! No-thing can hurt me!!"

It was quite a revelation, especially The Personal Power that this feeling of fearlessness afforded me. It gave me great clarity, and an absolute knowing without shadows of doubt, that in essence, *I am invincible; untouchable by anything in this world, even a fall from a great height.*

This *Empowered Presence* and Peace of Mind I was experiencing in the dream, then went on to help me face a situation (still dreaming) - to face a person instrumental in my childhood and with whom I experienced a lot of fear being the powerless child that I was back then. My father, a menacing figure most of the time, would oftentimes rage at me and say the most inappropriate and most cruel of things. In the situation in the dream, having regained that Power and Knowing, I did not fear him anymore and, in that fearlessness, I was able to speak my truth and take and claim that Power back.

The moral of the story: ***There is nothing to fear; only the idea of fear itself and the particular ways we conceptualise it and clothe it.***

It is still a Truth and a Power that I am learning and remembering to embody all the more, especially living in a world such as this. One which constantly and daily feeds us humongous amounts of fear dressed in the grandest of illusions.

So, keep your love-light on and shining, remembering as this quote **RE**-minds,

I used to be afraid of the dark until I learned that I Am The Light and the dark is afraid of me. - D. R. Silva

On Coming From Core:
Moment To Moment Meditation:
The Centre of Almighty Being

*January 2019 - The year before the Covid-19
pandemic struck.*

So, one of my resolutions this year is, , more often than not,
coming from my *Centre of Being*. I do not make resolutions
just for the New Year. Since forever self-realisation has
very much been a part of me and how I live. I have always
been Spiritually driven to, and take immense pleasure in,
making a fine art out of anything. For as long as I can
remember, I truly enjoy arriving at the *Inherent Inner
Beauty* of a thing and being committed to releasing the
unique fragrance it comes to give.

Since being on this *Self-Realisation Path,* one which began
in 1986, I have never gotten bored or tired of making my
Life, and its Expression, my most cherished and prized
work of HeArt. And I never tire of extending this same

dedication and commitment in my work with my counselling clients, on their individual and unique Life Journeys.

Like my 6-year solid meditation practice, **coming back** to Centre is an intention I have decided this day to apply to my every day; to apply to each activity and movement I am engaged in. It is the same dance of my sitting meditation, only meditation in action, and so much more than 'mindfulness.' This centring I am engaged in goes, sets and sits, that bit more *deep*.

Thus far, this Centring Practice, and this growing Inside-out experience of finding ground in being and root in **RE**-newal, has truly been an eye opener - a spiritual eye opener for a number of reasons. Firstly, because I am truly ready to take my spiritual and personal growth to that level and, as I am doing so, I am realising how much my sitting meditation has helped me; has helped me to know I can keep coming back repetitively when I come off track. That has been an eye opener which in turn makes me know, without doubt, that I can live in that more centred way and at that level of depth. It has been an eye opener seeing this and seeing that I know what I am doing. Secondly, it gives me a confidence that strengthens and sharpens my focus and resolve. I am loving this feeling of being more 'Inside-out' *unified;* much more complete and whole in a way I have never experiencd before.

Already it is making me feel more Inner Power and Peace and making me feel and believe I CAN DO ANYTHING; making me feel further skilled in The Art Of Creativity and Self-Mastery, which can only get better and better. This new development is making me feel that I can more fully *embody* and live under the tutelage of the following affirmation; one that, through mental and verbal reciting, has helped Call me back to the ground of Personal Power:

I am Beautiful, Peaceful, Confident and Powerful.

Which now reminds me of a quote from Alice Walker-

Every small positive change we make in ourselves, repays us in confidence in the future.

I have been hiding my fire and light under a bushel for way too long. I want to fully live. I want to fully shine. It is not a want, it is now most definitely a NEED.

I am ready to shine and enjoy the experience of shining, rather than dimming my light down and out. I want to release the fear that being myself in that more total way is dangerous and will unwittingly bring to me another's biting envy. In my life, I have had more than my fair share of that kind of back-biting from others. At those times, for the life of me, I could not figure out, or see, why me. Instead, I rationalised there must be something wrong with me because it kept happening and all I was doing was being myself. So, I am truly appreciating where I am finding myself at this moment in Time, Eternal.

What I have described so far is one side of this Centring Experience. The other side is that it is bloody hard at times to remain Centred, and continuously come back to Centre, as I move through my day and interact with people. Which reminds me of another quote that says words to this effect:

I was doing very well keeping and maintaining my centre and peace. Then I left the house.

The good thing about being more consciously and intentionally centred, is that I can immediately feel when I am about to be pulled *off-centre*. And there are so many bloody triggers!

My experience with regard to this running off and coming back to Centre, can be very much likened to the movement in any habitual behaviour pattern we try to dismantle. First comes the making of the decision, say to give up smoking cigarettes, then as you make your move with that decision, very soon realising and more clearly coming to see the exact life situations you tended to use cigarettes to self-soothe; discovering the myriad of ways cigarette was being used, every day, to cope, especially when shit gets difficult!

Currently, the biggest trigger I experience is at work, in my role as a counselling coordinator. Working within voluntary organisations, employees can find themselves being driven to work extra hard to maintain those services' provisions. Working tirelessly, 24/7, to ensure that the work is carried out to an exceptional standard, so that data can clearly demonstrate, annually, that the much-needed service and its provisions have a place in the community they serve. As a result, this becomes the focus of the organisation, often at the expense of the person-centered needs of the service user, and those employed to help them.

In becoming more centred I am releasing the trauma of the original people-pleaser part in me who feels the misplaced need to get work perfect, and, in so doing, inadvertently runs me rugged just to make everyone happy. Now, at work, all I allow myself to do is my very best, and most definitely leave the rest (which at this current workplace, is not making me flavour of the month!) See 'Wisdom At The Bottom Of The Pile' in Part Five.

Then there's the 'commuting experience' and releasing the temptation there to take others to task in so very many ways. Loads of triggers there, especially underground. But I am determined not to give My Power away. I can see more clearly now that when I do give my power away, the satisfaction of taking people to task only last a second or two, but long-term, it all builds up and exhausts me. All these little and often emotional withdrawals add up over-time. I'd rather keep *here-and-now energy free* and sweet and release the unconscious need to be 'drawn in' and pulled Off-Centre. That trance is no longer for me.

I'm loving it mostly, although in some situations it's hard and takes immense resolve to not get caught up in negative interactions, which include *inner derailing of personal thoughts and emotions*. Not forgetting to mention, the triggers in 'home life' and the many varied roles in the world of domestics any individual may occupy! But, I say again, I am determined because I know the fruits of this labour are going to be more than worth it, what with the immediate feel-good benefits I am already experiencing in the moment.

So, 4 days in and I am *strong and riding ready!*

A word of caution, **don't let the struggle become your identity..**

We are more than our struggles, so much more, and I absolutely don't mind sharing that good news through the sharing of my own experiences, however risky and very difficult that at times still very much *feels*. The truth is, we have been awesomely made and as such are spiritually enriched and equipped to make good of any adverse/life experiences and situations. We all have that *something-*

inside-so-strong, that knows that we can make it.... The greatest sin in this world is that we don't know we have that *something inside.*

KNOW THYSELF.

This is the highest and greatest of all education: true *Self-knowledge.* It not only helps us to know and understand ourselves, but also others... the added and unexpected bonus.

The Mind is there to Serve us, not to run us rugged.

I leave you with a final quote:

> **To be nobody but yourself in a world which is doing its best, night and day, to make you everybody else- means to fight the hardest battle which any human being can fight; never stop fighting.** - E.E. Cummings.

It is a worthy fight, The Good Fight, that brings forth, and heralds more Light.

On The Gifts of Our Compulsions:
Well Springs Within

I am currently re-reading 'The Gift Of Our Compulsions' by Mary O'Malley. In a nutshell, the book encourages us to see our compulsions as gifts; gifts because if we can stay still enough to understand them, we would find that at the *heart and bottom of compulsion is a deep Wellspring waiting to fulfil and nourish us as no external thing ever truly can.* No compulsion can give us the relief that we deep down need, nor even the relief we initially experienced when we first engaged in the compulsive behaviour. And it is this very inability that makes the activity compulsive, as it can never reach the underlying legitimate need, although it tries and tries and tries to.

Finding relief in compulsions is a bit like expecting to eat a banana to quench your thirst when it is a drink that the body needs; the banana quenching your thirst is never going to happen. Indeed, the only thing the banana can do is temporarily distract you from how thirsty you are. You can't fool the body, although we can spend our whole lifetime trying. The body knows what it needs and will come back to get it. The body is well equipped at doing its job and is as equally committed to it. And its job? Keeping us well and strong, across the board. We give the body very little credit for this. Both we and the world very easily turn the body into 'enemy' and then go on to treat it pretty badly, like it is a robot without feeling.

In Mary O'Malley's book we are also encouraged to not only change the way we view compulsions, but also to *change the way we relate to them,* bringing the light of much needed understanding and compassion to them. We must appreciate that they initially came into being to help us deal with and manage some great big difficult something. So, there's a way in which compulsions can be more readily resolved simply by seeing compulsions as more friend than foe - a treatment that also takes the sting out of them.

Compulsions come to go, being set up to serve us at one time and not for all our lifetime. The process of allowing them to pass is not an easy one considering the condition of compulsion's misunderstood heart. Not easy, but possible.

Compulsive behaviours are all kinds of addictions, like gambling, alcohol and substance misuse, all forms of eating disorders (including compulsive eating), overworking, keeping busy, surfing the net, social media, shopping, pornography, gaming... the list is exhaustive.

In the book the author offers many simple suggestions and exercises to help begin and engage the process of dismantling compulsion. The exercise I will share here with you is her idea of keeping a **Self-Awareness Diary.**

A Self-Awareness Diary

Get yourself a diary and divide the page into 3 columns. At the top of the first column write: *What is taking place now?* In the second column write: *What is happening with my compulsion?* And, on the top of the third column write: *What am I experiencing inside?*

My compulsive behaviour (of unconscious choice) from my early teens to mid-twenties was comfort eating, which developed into Bulimia. My healing journey began when I went into therapy for the eating disorder. Currently I am not bulimic and do not compulsively eat so much. What I sometimes still do is emotionally eat, sometimes eating foods that have no real nutritional content and value but, in the moment, attempt to rescue me from difficult situations and feelings, like compensating myself for doing too much at the expense of my own life energy.

This feeling of *too much* comes up often in my demanding job. It is also a role that is one of emotionally giving out; emotionally giving out and therapeutically and metaphorically *holding* survivors of traumatising domestic violence. Outside of work, I also have a couple of other challenges on my plate that take from me in similar ways, such as now being a carer for my adult son.

It is a testimony of how far I have come in my general healing journey, as well as in my recovery from disordered eating, that I have not fallen back into bulimia's misguided and crippling embrace because, like I said, currently -and ongoing for a good few years now- there is good enough reason to fall back into struggles with food. In the old eating disorder days, I would have binged and purged for less... Progress!!

Anyway, with the current, occasional, emotional eating I sometimes engage in, overall I have a good handle on it. However, this past week at work my self-awareness diary entry would have gone like this:

First column: The Situation - the pressures of work, especially after working with a highly anxious and traumatised client.

Second column: After meeting with this client, I noticed the need for something sweet, reassuring, and rewarding. I felt an ancient hungering and need for compensation. Indeed, an absent colleague had left a packet of sweet oat biscuits on her desk right beside me, and I felt those biscuits. That is I felt compulsion, tauntingly calling me, with its false comforting promises of self-soothing. *"There, there. Eat. Our treat."* Within the light of self-awareness, I consciously felt, and in so doing released, the temptation to emotionally eat. I am now more able to sit with compulsion without, reactively and immediately taking the decision to eat my wariness.

Third column: I can sit with the feeling of emotional drain, coupled with the feelings of tired and overwhelm - feelings already in the counselling room belonging to the client and being experienced by me in counter-transference. Similar feelings that I am also currently experiencing in my own ongoing and challenging life situations. I can now sit with these feeling states, as well as with the *'sucked dry'* bodily sensation of exhausted inner tensions.

And being well on the recovery road, like I have already mentioned, I can tolerate and contain that kind of internal angst, and delay. I do not engage those inner compulsive drives in a way I never could at the beginning of giving bulimia up. I know that these difficult and painful feeling states can and do pass, and I am now more familiar with the felt experience of their transmutation. *So, I no longer stand in Process' way because the reward and relief gained from this level of self-acceptance and self-awareness feeds and sustains me better than compulsively acting out ever did, or ever could, or ever will.*

I am re-reading Mary O'Malley's book because I am feeling challenged on a number of fronts and I want to ensure that compulsion don't try to sneak in through internal, unconscious, back doors. I want to keep that bolt on because my struggles do not need, or deserve, more suffering added on!

With regard to self-care, I do all those mind body spiritual things to keep me well. I exercise, meditate, eat healthily, live more in the moment and have greater self-appreciation and self-presence. These past 6 weeks, I have also taken to gifting myself with a *PJ stay-in-bed-all-day Saturday*. Even this is an achievement in and off itself because another one of my compulsions has been 'overdo and keep busy.' Initially I had found taking this particular monkey off my back, and simply being and relaxing, painstakingly angst-filled and mind-numbingly boring. Now that **IN**-sperience has been mostly transformed.

All is a Process and takes time. It has taken me 35 years to be where I am, as well as to fully realise that the nourishment and the joy is in *the journey itself,* not the destination. So, try not to worry yourself too much because, as such, we already have all the time in the world that we need and don't have to wait 'until' some future date to truly *enjoy* our lives and ourselves. To quote the author,

I am not offering you a cure. That is the old style of thinking in which your healing happens sometime in the future. This process is about inviting you into relationship with what is right now, (difficult or otherwise) for that is where true healing lies.

So, for those of you reading this and being not too long on *Transformation Road,* try keeping a Self-Awareness Diary and see the lessons and wisdom it draws to you. Keep the diary somewhere that you can make notes on what is happening both inside your body and out, throughout the day. For example, if your compulsion is with eating, keep the diary on the table in the kitchen. This exercise, and *all good attention given to ourselves in this more compassionate and curious way,* is exactly what is needed in the very moment we reach for our particular compulsive escapes...

Much like a child reaching to be picked up by her mummy and be given 'lap-time,' which probably was the kind of thing that was missing or lacking when compulsion first entered the scene, just like that mother we need to reach down in those moments, pick ourselves up and respond to our needs in more loving, nurturing and appropriate self-soothing ways.

Indeed, think about that day when you first engaged the now problem behaviour... What did you really need at that time? What were you hoping the behaviour could give you that you weren't getting? Is the penny dropping...? Before we can successfully change consciousness, we need to first raise consciousness through self-awareness and self-understanding.

Beneath every behaviour there is a feeling. And beneath each feeling is a need. And when we meet that need, rather than focus on the behaviour, we begin to deal with the cause, not the symptoms. - Ashleigh Warner.

Nothing has changed in the sense that these unmet needs are still there in need of the right attention and care. And when you start giving attention to yourself in this more self-caring way, the self-awareness diary will help to shed light on the things in your life causing ongoing unhappiness and strife... inviting compulsion in. And in bringing all what ails you to attention, *we are then called to do what needs being done to remedy the situation, even if that is simple acceptance.* Acceptance of the truth of how situations in our lives currently are and where we are with compulsivity.

We must discover new ways to better change and lovingly rock and hold those things in our lives that make us truly uncomfortable. And, as we do so, may we live more assuredly in Peace and its Serenity, and move toward our individual and collective lands of sweet milk and honey, more and more living the Life Imagined.

On Minding The Creative Gap:

Presence In Absence...

In your absence is your presence. - Jean Klein

I came across the above quote this week and it really resonated with me, especially with regard to the challenge of quietening my mind and giving it the space to *recline* and take that much needed time out of mind. Sometimes, it is genuinely hard to cultivate this mind-set; this **mind-centred-set,** if you like. At times, I am aware of my choosing to stand in my own way by wanting to seek refuge in my mind in the old ways. I can feel a reluctant part of me wanting to cling to old habits, and another part of me wondering if I should intervene or not, even in light of my wanting more Peace of mind and Clarity in thought.

The good news is, in the midst of all this, and my observance of it, there is that potent Creative Space; there is this Pause, this Gap, where one can make life-changing decisions. A Space filled with the *Inner rich pickings of possibilities.*

Even if, in that moment, the unconscious wins out, there is this Space being created where the light of consciousness is beginning to have more Presence and cover more ground - the beginning of the end of the old ways is at hand. When there is more Presence, there is such Peace and Quiet; like the sun finally breaking through on an initially grey and cloudy day, and the welcomed warmth that sunshine brings, that feels so wonderful on the skin - on one's very Being.

And out of that clear blue sunny sky come the *awesome thoughts belonging more to Divine Mind* - if you have ever experienced that or believe in such a concept. This is the place where *In*sights and *In*spiration seem to come 'out of the blue/ethereal' (out of the forever real). I think most of us have had this experience, this reveal-a-tion, at some point in our lives. We tend to keep experiences like this to ourselves due to fear of rejection and judgement, where spirituality is seen as 'weird' and unscientific, therefore irrelevant nonsense. It is no wonder that we have a problem with our own spirituality and all things spiritual too; keeping spirituality closeted.

God, whose Love and Joy are present everywhere, can't come to visit you

unless you aren't there. - Angelus Silesius

Take a moment... have you ever had one of those moments when your mind emptied-out and you heard/felt/saw something new, however fleeting, which could not have made its presence felt without you being absent-minded in this way? Without you being *all-taken-up in thought and its mostly repetitive contents?* Creatives/artists/survivors-becoming-thrivers pay particular attention to these moments and attempts to capture and record them, as I am doing here.

Oftentimes we are so attached to our thoughts to the extent that we believe *every single thing we think,* without even thinking to check our thoughts against reality. Sometimes we are so attached to our thoughts that we don't let anything new in, or out; we don't open the curtain of the closed mind and let in a little sunshine.

Most of the great and advancing ideas that have brought amazing things into existence in this world have come out of this absence of being so full of ourselves, the world, and its contents. I believe that some of us are more temperamentally designed to have easier access and privy to this **IN**-Tuition, eg. Fringe-dwellers. We can all learn to cultivate and fine tune this Gift, as human beings we have that capacity... dare we give it the attention it needs to develop and grow.

Many are called, but few choose to listen... few choose to IN-tuit...

For example, some of you are going to totally get what I am trying to say here, while others are going to think I am speaking total gobbledygook, and that is okay. Maybe I am... who is truly to say? Who can truly have the last word on these things, as we are only on this earth plane in the blink of galactic eyes.

All I know is all I know, and all I know, I know through my experiences and the pearls of wisdom that have come out of those experiences as I attempt to make good on a deep desire to remain awake, live to potential, and have the best life experience humanly possible. This desire drives my life, and...

As our desire is, so is our will. As our will is, so is our deed. As our deed is, so is our destiny...

All I know is that, even though a part of me is terrified of creating that Space and allowing for that kind of self-absence, when I take that Leap of Faith, following the initial aftershocks, there is no denying The Peace, The Bliss, The Sweet Serenity that this kind of emptying-out brings. And in that Space, I *RE*-member that the void, the empty, the unknown, is not scary at all; that this kind of emptiness and absence triumphs over the traumatic emptiness that grows out of childhood wounds of significant loss.

In this Space, there is deep healing and the kind of comfort & reassurance found in the unconditional loving arms of a mother rocking her frazzled and over tired baby to sweet Surrender and dreams... there's nothing like it.

But, alas, it takes time to convince the whole of me (and get the whole of me!) on side. It is so compelling and tempting to slip back into unconsciousness, into ignorance being bliss, especially when I run into old obstacles, like over-extending myself and not taking due rest - that is my Achilles' heel. I can still inadvertently overwhelm myself by taking on way too much, emotionally and otherwise.

Success is a journey, not a destination. - Ben Sweetland

I need to continue to harness The Power of Patience and learn how to enjoy the Journey that bit more, if only to ensure Presence does not get lost and **RE**-placed with living in the future of *"When this or that gets better, THEN this or that will happen;"* like happiness and fulfilment. Happiness is to be had now, knowing how wonderfully benevolent true life actually is. The reward is to be discovered Here and Now. The Joy is to be tasted **Here and Now.** Peace is to be experienced Here and Now.

The Time is Now...

On Rocky Roads:
Love Drives Divine, All Ways

Give your mind the SPACE it needs, and
it will serve you tirelessly. - Unknown

Okay, so two weeks into Resolutions Intentioned for this year and beyond - those *IN*-tentions essentially being The *Ongoing Dream* of More Peace of mind, More Peace, Joy, Truth and Love in my life, alongside Acceptance *with* and *in* my life situations - I ran into a wall. A wall that I did manage to get over... just about.

The resolution of coming from Centre and moving myself out the way long enough to make *The Land of Dreams* continue to come through and work out for me, along with a mindset that can work for me tirelessly and optimally, is truly throwing up all that being Off-Centre had unconsciously and habitually tried to hide and mask.

At the level of Mind, I am realising that endeavouring to move through the day and generally just live and be more Centred, means releasing the need to escape and get lost in *thought patterns*.

I love my world of thoughts - it has been a great escape of mine; broadening my mind, playing with ideas, entertaining myself, thinking whatever I like... learning as much as I can. But this week I saw and *felt more clearly and keenly* that I have to get a hold on my thoughts and its more unhelpful roads, just like the hold I have cultivated during 6 years of consistent meditation, although I have been meditating on and off for decades.

Meditation is thought-freeing rather than *old thought pattern mind-imprisoning* that holds you hostage and takes you clear and way out off the ground of *Here and Now*. However challenging my situation has gotten, and however I may get temporally caught up in mind-imprisoning thought patterns, I know I can do it: I know I can keep coming back, and that in itself is quite encouraging and **RE**-configuring.

I like, love, and prefer, **living, moving, and having My Being, There. Here. Now.**

There is a saying that goes,

> *'Be careful what you wish for; you might get it.'*

204

Getting it requires a lot of adjustment, concentration and unlearning - a process that cannot be rushed. It has its own Divine Timing.

What I am **RE**/learning to do as I am in the midst (and material mist) of life, is not to absent-mindedly follow every thought, to not get too entangled up, and to generally be more careful about the kind of thoughts I entertain, because they can truly take me off-track. All this has been a key realisation this week, as well as seeing, for myself, how allowing myself to run away with my thoughts has a direct impact on my 'Inner world of feelings and thoughts.' Being mindless in thought can contribute toward my emotions running riot, which makes my feelings grow troublesome, and in so doing, my Inner Peace and Joy fade away and get replaced by 'moodiness.'

My emotions, I liken here to being like a child in a big department store, losing hold of her mother's hand; getting lost and emotionally upset, only knowing Inner Peace once more, when mother and child are reunited. This is how the relationship between my mind and emotion has been, and the contentious dance of to-ing and fro-ing, as I attempt to herald in more wholesome lasting life changes. Indeed, as I am writing this, I am reminded of this dream I get every so often, where I get lost and frantically try to get back from whence I first came - back home to familiar ground.

What I am learning this week is that my mind needs to be Centred and that, in itself, is quite a discipline. I *RE*-membered that, when my mind is more Centred, the Inside-out Peace and Joy that comes with it and envelopes my existence, is more than worth it...

It is worth the dancing (and at times wrestling!) with the *human being physical existence experience.* The struggle is real, *being IN this world, though not totally OF it.*

Oftentimes it is much easier to control and interrupt thoughts than it is *RE*-storing calm in the emotional - especially once the cat has been let out of the proverbial bag; unsettling is the way it has to be as part of life and life's Elevation Process. And when the situation, whether it be in thought or external reality, triggers old stuff from one's traumatic past, then *RE*-storing calm can take days... weeks... months... years... *depending on the depth and breadth of the trauma, the resilience of its captor, and whether there were any nurturing and kind adults around during that childhood time.*

So, for the likes of me, a day or two is a great improvement because at the beginning of my recovery and Self-*RE*-discovery Journey, when I had less IN-sight, Self-under - *and Inner* -standing and Healing, Peace and Being *RE*-stored, took loads longer.

This week for me the most triggering situation was at work, with being new in a post - a position that comes along with its more than fair share of pressures, and great expectations. This bears some resemblance to my childhood, where I felt very much thrown in at the deep end and was expected to know what I was doing, without being taught. And not only know what I am doing, but also to not make mistakes if I didn't want to get a cussing.

Such *old familial experiences* as these, trigger the need to put back in place early conditioning reactive thought and behaviour patterns, as ways of coping with emotional trigger and overwhelm. The *old escape* used to be becoming obsessive in thought about my life situations, trying to work and figure things out, *up there*. The old familial escape of overthinking about whether I am eating too much; worrying that I am eating the wrong kind of stuff, triggering that angst-filled mental state of fat feeling. Of feeling fat and ugly. Of feeling worthless, love-starved, and undeserving, especially of good things happening to and for me. Reaching out for comfort in food as I can feel pulled to do, although I am happy with the handle I now have on this particular coping mechanism.

These are aspects of the-cat-that-needs-to-be-let-out-of-the-bag, and beared, as part and parcel of *maintaining a certain Centre AND being grounded in my body* - whatever the 'imagined weight'; wherever, whenever and with whatever I may be lost in thought with.

During childhood, living mostly up in my head was a much better place to be than living on solid ground in a

70% pain-filled, out-shaping reality. It can be a lifelong walk on this Road of Becoming. Becoming all that you may be, outside of and through adverse childhood experiences...

If this is you too, *you are doing great,* like me! And, like me, feel free to claim further greatness, deeper healing, and self *RE*-Discovery.

Keeping doing and enjoying this way of life, daily, is *My Great Everything,* added to the difference-making that can be taken (and sweet-lemonade-making) from sharing my life journey. This way of living and being is the good job I jump up to every morning eager to RE-do and enjoy, again and again! *The Great Sun Joy God* who *RE-*igns Sun Rays (aka INNERLIGHT) on Planet Earth and all who inhabit Her sphere, brightens my *Innerside-out* world. Life, my life, our life, made out of love; coming forth from love, day by day.

So, I will hold still and learn, *knowing* that Life is filled with Grace, and these initially painful emotional waves will pass; just like day passes, to give way to night... in service to Light, the guide that is Love.

Every day I am committed to using *whatever comes my way,* to brighten up the day.

And I'll let you into a little secret....

Obstacles don't block The Path, they are The Way!!

And to quote Carl Jung:

The psychological rule says that when the intra situation is not made conscious, it happens outside, as fate.

Meaning, Peace and Harmony with *IN*, Peace and Harmony with *OUT*...

Love The Light. Love Your Life. Love **RE**-sides in All Ways and Areas of life, *emerging* forth into The Light, day by day by day. Love drives Divine, *All Ways*. So, find Your Way: Love *wills it* will be okay.

POEM: On The Cost of Change:

Exchange

A lot of people are always begging for Change,
but are afraid of Change,
because Change means
you must give something up -
cos that's what you owe
when Change's got your back.

An integral being knows without going, sees without looking, and accomplishes without doing. - Lao Tzu

Part Five: Unprecedented

Even The Darkest Night Will End And The Sun Will Rise. - Rumi

There is a necessary pain that comes with change... personal and collective. This applies in our personal as well as collective lives as a people and as a species. Oftentimes people want change without changing themselves or their lives in any shape or form; scared as humans are of experiencing the discomfort that change initially for a time brings... But that is how change works, and all life is subject to change. We are not just here to sunbathe & be comfortable... We are here to Grow

and Evolve. We Are Life In Human Form. We must learn to Humane-Up for the sake of our souls, the planet, and human life form continued existence on the planet.

- Denise James

POEM: Birth Rites

I feel flushed, lush like -
a newly formed butterfly
coming into flight;

Liberated like, a recently adjudicated
Eve, freed, running bare feet, off
 into pastures green - unafraid
to give into Inner promptings.

I feel wickedly creative, like the Virgin
Mary; fruitfully making babies, with such ease -
just like a breeze.

Dare I Take a bite and give into Grand Appetite,
Seen as I'm feverishly ripe, bursting at the seams,
in urgent need of gentle, manly, tender feelings
running river deep?

I just might, because it ain't no Lie,
for the longest of time I've been dying to live
a life undeniably Satisfied,

As the good Lord was when
She first tasted Life.

On Living The Life Imagined:

Seek Ye First The Queendom of Love

Okay, 2020 is upon us... though the time is always *Now o Clock*. I have some big developments taking place in 2020. The biggest, wildest, dreamiest being, the publication of my book, **'Back to Love'**; back from what I was taught was love, to what love very simply *IS*. It has been some kind of journey unlearning that *mis-education* and setting myself on the right path *Life called out for me*.

The Journey for me has been a bit like deciding to change a room around, to give it a different look, perspective and feel; then 2-4 hours into it, finding oneself knee deep in *stuff* and the whole place looking totally upside down. Standing there, in the thick of it, seriously wondering if you should have started making this change to begin with! Wondering if all this mess is worth it but being too far gone to turn back and change back now... deciding to keep on, until the work is done - whenever that is!! Keep on keeping on, inspired by the vision of how much more **life-giving** and **life-affirming** the change will be, and have you *feel*.

That is what my book **'Back to Love'** is all about: that decision, its process, the mess, and the Dream of holding that *Call of Love's, 'Time for Change'*, a bundle of Joy, made in this time, possible.

Outside of my book, there are other continuing developments in the pipeline of my life of *having put a lot of hard work in, honing the skills required for longevity Dreams, that now await harvesting*. All this, whilst also working at striking a more happy and *much needed* wholesome *life-work* balance.

There are many pathways on this one road I am on. What is yours? What is your Dream?

Everybody's got a ***Thang... called by name to bring...*** in this one Life to live; each to their own... Love further blesses The Soul that's got its own.

More Life to us all as we seek first the Kingdom of Love, and all Her ways, and in so doing and being, have all our hearts desires added on, too! Hallelujah!!

On Being True to Self:
Authenticity Deficiency Disorder
(A.D.D)

Earlier today I was listening to Elizabeth Lesser's book, *'Marrow'*, and I just had to share something I read there that resonated with me. Before I do, I want to share that every book I read - that I reach out to read or it finds me - comes when I am facing something that is challenging in my life and that is calling me to further growth and self-understanding. I loved Elizabeth Lesser's book, *'Broken Open'*, which I read maybe 15 years or so ago. Her soul speaks to and resonates with mine in an effortless and easy manner.

During Covid-19 and its sudden prevalence of high death rates, especially back in March and April 2020, and having experienced the loss of loved ones losing loved ones, I felt the need to make Peace, again, with death; with this twin that comes with human and earthly life, which we humans find hard to accept and live with, let alone entertain when it comes knocking. I very much wanted to find a way to quell the fear in the world and the fear in my every day, so off I went searching for the *right (now)* book.

In her book *'Marrow'* where Lesser is growing through the experience of losing her sister to cancer, she asserts that in this contemporary world today, most of us are suffering from **ADD: Authenticity Deficiency Disorder.** I agree. I believe that this world and its inhabitants have a supreme case of *Authenticity Deficiency Disorder,* and the capitalist materialistic world we live in encourages that. I also believe that death scares us so because we are not living an Authentic life and we are not being our Authentic Self, and in so doing not living to potential. Being who we are - outside the opinions of others - is what we are here to be and do; not to be carbon copies, not to solely be what the world tells us is acceptable. *We are, and we have, Agency.*

Isn't that what deathbed regrets are full of...? Life **UN**-lived woulda, coulda, shouldas...

Let your Authentic Light shine bright...

The world, like never before in our time, needs *Your* Light and needs *Your* Unique and particular *difference-making* superpower gift. Your precious beating heart may be the exact thing someone's aching Soul needs; might be the exact thing we are being Called in lockdown to **RE**-discover and do better. Yes. **You.** Who you are truly, uniquely. *You,* of which there is your **only one copy.** Nature, Creation, only deals in *Originals.*

We *belong,* to Life, and as such, Life has created space and a place for us – **all** - here in this world. So, take Your place, Centre Stage, within and outside your life, to be fully cured of this particular kind of ADD.

On Loving Our Neighbours
As Ourselves:
Our Brother's Keeper

Just passing by to say, let's not turn on each other for finding a safe way to do exercise if that is what keeps us mind body spirit well. I've been going to the park and jogging. I am lucky because I have two parks walking distance from me. I can struggle with PTSD anxiety so need this outlet. Children also need exercise which can be done safely in the park. Some of us do not have gardens. Also, some of us have already been living and exercising this sense of *Social Responsibility* - aka *Collective Responsibility*, way before Covid.

Social/Collective Responsibility is one of **Kwanzaa**'s Key Principles. Kwanzaa is a festival observed by many Africa Americans from 26th December to 1st January as a celebration of cultural heritage and traditional values. Kwanzaa also helps to build up black folks Personal and Collective self-esteem and self-confidence, especially via

RE-learning about our true history and being encouraged to take that Sankofa Journey back to true living and being. Some Black British people practice and observe Kwanzaa too on these side of the shores. I am one of those.

During this time of Covid I've been banging on that, yes, we are indeed our Brother's Keeper. It is going to take self-absorbed people that bit longer to grasp this - and some will still behave irresponsibly.

Before Covid-19 we had been living in a world increasing going back into the dark ages of hatred, believing it is alright to spread and act out that be-devilling spirit. Being a counsellor in the business of change, change doesn't happen overnight, and change doesn't happen unless it is wholeheartedly wanted. The individual must be looking straight in the eye of the problem before beginning that Journey Of Maturation.

We still need *Love*, under- and Inner-standing and *rude awakenings*. That was the case before the Coronavirus and will continue to be the case for all humans on Planet Earth.

One of my favourite ancient African Philosophy says, which very much applies today like never before,

Whatever happens to the individual, happens to the whole group, whatever

***happens to the whole group, happens to
the individual.***

It's human, and okay, to feel vulnerable and afraid, but let us try extra hard to keep love and conscientiousness in the driving seat of our lives, not fear and division. Also remember to keep an eye on, and steer clear of, that bedevilling spirit of divide and rule - it loves such times as these! Nuff said...

On Waking Up:
Whilst The Iron's Hot

Kinda feeling like the Earth just sent us all to our rooms to think about what we've done.

I kinda agree...

On that score there is no one exempt at this Pandemic Coronavirus time; the privileged cannot buy their way out, the racist can't use the poisonous 'we are superior" card. At this time, it has been made crystal clear - the world over - that we are One People, One Planet Earth, One Human Race. All indoors at this time, being asked to re-think our time and place on this planet and to set our priorities straight: to *come again* if we are to continue well-enough on this Earth Plane, on loan to us whilst we are here. It belongs to no one!

Hopefully we will listen this time, as I know that *many are called,* but historically thus far, *few choose to listen.*

Another quote says,

It is not a question of when mankind will learn; but when mankind will act on what it already knows.

It is time to listen; it is time to act on what, in our hearts, souls and minds, *we know.*

As mentioned previously, before Coronavirus we had been living in a world politically increasingly going backward in time, slipping into hatred and believing it is alright to spread and act out that be-devilling spirit.

And here **we all are,** locked down in our homes, with *Social Responsibility,* aka *Collective Responsibility* and the spirit of *Co-operation,* becoming new buzz words. All of a sudden, we are all expected to know how to behave more just and fair: to live all together as one. This is how life should have been to begin with. Minorities have known and shouted for this the longest!

People, it's time to *awake;* it's time for that *new paradigm* to take its place. The old-world order no longer works. Look where it has got us... a dis-eased earth, a broken physical environmental world, this Coronavirus time with fear and terror running rampantly amok....

There have been sooo many Coronavirus related deaths; sooo many dying alone. Loved ones not able to be with family and friends when they sadly draw their last breaths. Friends and loved ones not able to go say goodbye at funerals; the vulnerable, once again, being the ones most impacted. People, **WE NEED TO GET THIS!!**

So, whilst *we are all doing Time*, it is *Time o' Clock* to try something new and move away from the ill-advised materialistic view, and listen more to the kind of people Melissa Kennedy speaks of in the following quote,

> *We need to encourage the quiet rebels, the ones with a Cause burning deep inside. For once they find a way to let the truth out of their bones, they just may bring the whole earth to bloom.*

Wonderful.

That's me. A not so quiet any more Rebel.

So, whilst a lot of things in our lives at this time have been cancelled, let's more firmly reinstate, and *lift on high, love and understanding*. These two remedies the planet desperately needs – this has been the case way before Coronavirus and will continue to be the case for us as a species going forward.

NB: (Directly after the end of the worse of Covid, on 24th February 2022, Ukraine and Russia went to war, that became the ongoing bad news. Lord of Love, Mother of God, help us!)

And to those of you already woke, more Power to you; keep spreading *The Light* of Peace, Joy, Truth and Love.

To those of you currently woken-enough not to fall back - more Power to you also.

To those of you still preferring an ignorance that is no longer bliss, Rude Awakenings to you! And hopefully to you alone, as oftentimes the shady apple in a cart spoils it for us all, much like punishment being metered out by a teacher to a whole class because of the misbehaviour of one single person.

On Seeing It, All:
Wisdom At The Soul Bottom Of
The Pile

In relationships between dominant and subordinate groups, the subordinate group members always possess a far greater understanding of the dominant group members and their culture than vice versa. - Harriet G Lerner.

This week I heard, again, that Jamaica was the place slave owners placed the Africans who fought hard against slavery, from all the different countries that held Africans captive. It was thought and hoped by slave owners that these individuals of rebellious Africans (i.e. freedom fighters) would not fare well on what these slave owners saw as inhabitable highlands.

This makes me feel kinda proud... It makes me wonder if this is where my *tenacious spirit* comes from, as whenever something, or someone tries to knock me down, as a *grown and woke* Black Woman, I instinctively rise-up and stand up for myself, whoever the person in Western man-made hierarchy facing off against a Sister such as me maybe. I **RE**-present my ancestral self, unapologetically. I know the shoulders I stand on; that my life is built on.

I have *carried out my own independent investigation of the truth,* and who I am is definitely not what Euro-ego-centric mind sets have made me and my fellow original African black people. So, please allow me to correct you, when you stand in the line of needing correcting!

Being from that Black African subordinate group, who are able to see "*all angles*", I struggle with feminism; mostly because the founding feminists, who names themselves thusly, were white privileged women and they have an active history of being my oppressors and have not wrestled enough with that themselves - with that uncomfortable truth, still. Their prejudice is oftentimes unconscious and difficult for them to willingly recognise.

I have seen this prejudice in the workplace with some white women's dealings with me. I see this prejudice in their fear (however unconscious) of my assertiveness as a black woman and see how quick I get turned in their minds into "*angry black woman*" - an accusation unconsciously designed to get me on the defence and right back on track of *oppressor and oppressed/enslaved.* This is a reality to black folks, however unconsciously acted out and participated in by those who in misguided blindness hold tightly to Westernised world views, its historical untruths and constant society-feeding misinformation.

You, my feminist sister, you wanted to get out the house and go to work; we, your darker hues, longed to feel and be (financially and otherwise) comfortable and esteemed. To have had the choice to stay home and override having to do it all, the world made that a luxury for the likes of me. To stay at home, nurse our children, take them to and from school, that would have been wonderful! Heaven! *Ain't I a woman, too?*

You see, that four acres and a mule did not get us very far; some of us are still very much on historical catch up, just like someone coming from childhood adverse experiences, as adult, is psychologically catching-up too, emotionally and developmentally. Then you see me in the workplace, giving me aggro.

I have seen other minority groups, for example Asians from China and Asians from India, look down on black people from a heritage such as mine, only happy to include the likes of me and mine when they need the money from our pockets to line their own. Or when others, still, need our numbers to increase the power and force in their particular minority societal struggle; using us as it suits them, including politicians. How very useful we can be, until we ask, *"What about me?"* Until we say, *"You are wrong; kindly check yourself, at your earliest convenience."*

To me, the *True Feminist* has done the healing; has done the uncovering and recovery of privilege and that false sense of identity and security that comes with it. True Feminism has looked at, and understands, their internalised racism and the ways they hold dear to it when it suits them. Be open and human. Admit it. Admit your continued hold to privilege and the esteem you sneak from it, for you did not personally create it... we came here and found it. We can stop participating erroneously in it now. It's time. That's what makes *Woke*.

The *Truly Woke Feminist* can allow the black woman, wherever she finds her, to *Her Voice;* to hold feminism accountable when feminism starts to zone out and becomes unconscious, trying to fall into ignorance, which is far from bliss for your Black Sister.

The True Feminists have gone *off* themselves and done the work, instead of expecting black folks to teach them; instead of expecting black folks to open their eyes. In that moment of *opportunity knocking decision,* do something New World paradigm-needing-shifting different, other than the erroneous playing of the unconsciously preferred role of patriarchal victim. Until you can do this, your Cause will not be reflective of me and mine, at the bottom of the pile - far-seeing, far-reaching, truth-loving perspective.

Just like, to me, a True Christian is out in the world making waves; giving vent to legitimate anger when he or she sees ignorance masquerading like it's all learned! A True Christian, like Christ, is kicking down tables in synagogues, holding others accountable; putting themselves and their lives on the line, risking being crucified! Same too for true feminism; she is supposed to know how racism - from her own subjugated woman kind (though privileged) position - taste and feels... *and detest it.* She does not pick and choose injustice depending on whose company she is in in that moment: *she, like Christ, like me, like folks Woke, calls shit out, wherever shit is. Period!*

So, being a woman, in 2022, I do not feel myself to be a feminist - I don't believe that movement is totally for me and mine, not quite yet. Just like if Christ came back, He would kill himself, seeing what has happened and is being done in His name. The fight against injustice is inclusive; not temperamental, not sentimental, not momentary, not occasional. You have to roll up your sleeves and risk getting dirty deep in shit if you are a true fighter of injustice and freedom. At times you will not be liked; you will be laughed at, ostracised, crucified, burnt alive, hanged from a tree, scapegoated, continuously. But, however difficult, it still remains the place to Get Up, Stand Up, and Be At.

And with especial regards to the workplace, where this piece of writing is inspired, true feminism does not follow blindly patriarchal worn out and privileged policies and procedures. True Feminists are *every new day pioneers,* fighting the *Good Fight* inside and outside of work - not just Monday-Friday 9-5pm; the True Christian, not just on Sundays.

True Freedom Fighters of Injustice, also detest the straight jacket that is bound up in the word *"professional"*. In the workplace "being professional" oftentimes means being hard-hearted, without conscience; stepping on people you feel are beneath you and holding tight to hierarchy; leaving *feeling, Inner-tuition and emotion* out of the equation... most of which makes us human!

Maybe "being professional" should be replaced with statements such as *integrity, emotional intelligence, self-awareness, having conscience, kindness, cooperation...* being in *true nature*, each other's keepers, which makes us *true humans*, whatever place we may be doing that.

Maybe then institutions would not be a huge malignant world and a law unto themselves; oppressive toxic spaces, where all that is most humane has no place, and is oftentimes driven out, and the real bad bullying apples remain unchecked by *majority,* however minority these very bad apples may be. There's a lack of courage in toxic workplaces... and in the world.

I read a quote the other day that says,

People do not leave good workplaces; they leave toxic work cultures.

How very true... Toxic Cultures... bad bacteria... no Good coming forth from it.

The True Feminist understands when I get angry and does not use my (legitimate) anger against me. The True Feminist works hard at setting aside an unconscious negating envy that oftentimes becomes unnerved when I stand up for myself and assertively call out all things unjust, especially when I find it. Instead of getting defensive, The True Feminist will consider my **more all-seeing all-angle perspective**, being at that bottom of societal created manmade pile: a position *well-seasoned and experienced in* isms and kisms, misguided nonsense.

In 2022, during this season of racism *still alive and kicking revival,* I prefer to play with Bell Hooks ideas on feminists and feminism taken up in her 1981 book *"Ain't I a Woman? Black women and feminism."* Bell Hooks first gave me the window to articulate and view feminism and its relationship to the black woman, also taken up by Alice Walker in her idea of *'Womanism'.* These ideas, at this current time, are more *BE*-fitting to me.

We have come quite a way, but we still have some ways to go... to grow.

And so, to the white feminist, I say to you,

If you have come here to help me, you are wasting our time. But if you have

come because your liberation is bound up with mine, then let us work together.
- Lila Watson

From: A Righteously Angry, Articulate, Self-Loving Black/African Woke Woman....

NB: I left that toxic workplace and became self-employed. I resigned as soon as I saw the bullshit brewing, developing, and *progressing* in my direction. Alhough it was quite stressful running into that battle again, this time around it was a pleasure nipping it in the bud as swiftly as I did. I took the leap of faith and went totally self-employed and today I am doing very well there. That job was not going in my *life-affirming direction.* When travelling by the **Higher Way,** knowing and learning how and when to quit toxic work cultures is very important.

On The Courage of Happiness

I read a quote recently that said, **"Happiness is an act of courage,"** and I believe it is so. Following one's heArt and choosing Happiness, over and over, again and again, takes courage. Especially for those who have experienced Adverse Traumatic Childhood Experiences and those who experience trauma and loss as adults. We were made to be happy, and those who have suffered, deserve Happiness even more; happiness that is lasting, however much the various human life situations may temporarily cloud and block the warmth of that *Inside-out* feeling of a lasting Joy. Like the sun behind the clouds, Happiness and Joy, being the *more natural universe-harmonising homeostasis order*, is always there - in all ways, all places, and all challenges and mental states we may find our very human selves in.

As John Welwood reminds in his book *'Perfect Love Imperfect Relationships'*,

**The psychological work thins the cloud,
Spiritual work invokes the sun.**

On Following Your Bliss:
The Sparrow Of Lasting IS-ness
Happiness

Happiness became *more fully lit* and alive for me in August 2020 when Covid was at its heights. I realised, and the penny finally dropped, that just like I fight for, honour, and keep *my Inner Peace*, I can do likewise with *Lasting Happiness*. So, I decided to have that kind of relationship with Happiness. I decided to make and keep that commitment to Happiness. And, as wise souls have observed, the moment I made that decision earlier this week, *testy things* immediately begun to turn up, almost like they came to take back Happiness.

Then I remembered and calmed myself, having learned - and am always open to *learning from my experiences* - another commitment I have made some time ago - that those situations weren't tests; they weren't the devil trying to wrangle back some kind of control. In making the Happiness decision, in those habitual ways of thinking, behaving, seeing, being, living and loving, I was seeing right through the old defence. I saw how swiftly PTSD terror, trying to steal my portion of Joy, turned up, threatening *Lasting Happiness*, attempting to undermine and tarnish it.

Once upon a time, I needed those conditioned thoughts, feelings and behaviour patterns to survive and keep me psychologically alive... Once upon a time, it was safer living small. Safer keeping myself to myself, to safe-keep my Good and my Joy, as a child.

No matter what shows up in front of me, threatening to make me jump out of my skin, I am going to allow the *vulnerability* that comes with those human experiences. I am going to allow vulnerability and seek out proper comfort and safety. And, once calmed, I'm gonna choose Happiness, over and over and over. I am going to choose Happiness, over-all.

Yes, I will have emotions about stuff, both positive and negative ones. Just like the weather has all types of weather, I am going to have those, and at those times make a greater concerted effort to not "add to" my suffering. As Buddha believed, there is suffering that comes with living in the world, and then there is the (unnecessary) suffering we inadvertently add to that suffering; inadvertently adding to our pain.

The good news is, it is within our hands to lose that *"suffer some more"* add on... When Christ said The Kingdom is at hand, She wasn't lying...

All we have to do to **RE**-claim *more lasting Inside-out Happiness,* is move ourselves out of the way and let nature take and run Her course... more consistently. And when She is done, let Her get back on that Happiness Horse, taking us wherever She Wills and Wants: Her wherever is **all-ways**-good... whatever route you take with Lasting Happiness.

That Sun that **IN**-vokes spiritual Rays, has walked with me through dark nights and long days during my child-hood past. I *always felt* its Presence, that is how I *know* God, Love (whatever you may call it) is real. For me, no other explanation is needed for myself, and I can live like that without trying to convince others. This means *my* Spiritual Reality and Spiritual Life - and the Spirit that is me - means, and is, *everything* to me and to *my* overall optimal wellbeing.

Without this *Self-Knowing,* I cannot imagine how cold life itself would feel and be for the likes of me. Without this Self-Knowledge, I can imagine how cold and cruel the world is felt to be by some. Indeed, I have fell victim many times to those kinds of uncaring cold-feeling hands.

Without this moment-to-moment daily warmth of **IN**-side-out Happiness, needed for all life forms, we invite degeneration. Animals animate, no second guessing, while humans try to be everything other than who he or she truly is. This has been my *felt experience* and now Expanded Perspective. Take it or leave it, I do not force feed it. We are all in our individual and collective classrooms in this experience called Life, being **IN**-vited to truly Live and Learn from Experience and **RE-**member, our most true Self.

Although I have been a lone wolf most of my life, I know there is my pack, my tribe out there who hear this howl. Who feel this howl. I know I am not alone, however lonely and alone I may sometimes feel. I know I will still, at times, experience the clouding over of who I am, and I am thankful that I am much improved in riding the transient *This Shall Pass Too* storm, out.

So, here I am. This is me. More and more unapologetically coming out of this degenerative Western worldview. Here I am. *Daring to share* God-given talents. Here I am, grounded and rooted in **IS**-*ness* that brings more lasting Peace, Joy and Happiness.

On Coming Out The Spiritual Closet:

Out Coming

My Spirituality is **everything** to me. It saved my life; it kept me alive; it urges me to follow *my dreams*. Dreams which house my most true identity... the *that of why* I am here.

Here in this life, in this space, at this time. Here to share, so that those down by the river, waiting for the Good Love/Life to come their way, may have their thirst quenched and experience true healing and being, in this time.

In these times I am coming out more and more, in the unlimited potentiality of *awesomely and magnificently made.* I am coming forth day by day, having previously lost my Light to the bushel. In the Light, unapologetically, I am stepping *out...* now I *know,* who I am!

I Never Loose, I Either Win, Or Learn.

True Learning makes us, in all ways, on top of our game...
True Learning makes us woke and truly life aware. Makes
us humane human beings - *the kind of species we have
been **IN**-side-out wired to become.*

Come out from the Bushel Closet. ***Stop Shading Your
Shine:*** Real Life and True Living very much minds!

On Daring Greatly:
Soul In The Arena

I am here on a Sunday afternoon, 4pm on June 28th 2020, watching a documentary on American professor, Brenè Brown. I love what she has to say on the relationship between *Vulnerability and Courage,* most poignant, that there is strength in vulnerability. Her words have the right *IN-formation energy* for me to be receiving at this time, as I prepare to step out on the "getting my book, *Back to Love,* published" road.

All the while whilst writing my book, (and rewriting it and re-editing it), over these very many years, vulnerability has sat very close beside me wondering, "What the fuck are you doing!? Are you really serious about getting this book published?! To have it out there in the world? This cruel world!?!"

Last year, all the *nothing ever happens before the time* ducks were in line when Sèan Patrick, Founder and CEO of 'That Guy's House (TGH)' publishing company (now 'The Good House'), made his appearance in my life, at Opportune Time. And now that dream, **'Back to Love'**, is set on becoming a reality. And being as close as it is to reality, vulnerability and high anxiety are running riot inside of me, afraid of backlash, mostly afraid of the outside, *Armchair Critic*.

But watching Brenè Brown's film, especially the part where she quotes from Theodore Roosevelt's 1910 address speech, I know that this moment has not happened by chance, and I am as ready as I will ever be to respond to this book getting published - *call to courage*.

I am so incredibly proud of myself and so thankful for this Journey that has given my Life Meaning, Passion and Purpose, keeping my Peace, Truth, Joy and Love Tank full-enough up: Humane, Up.

I will allow the haters their hate; their hate ain't none of my business, least of all what they think. I will allow the critics their snigger. I will allow the cynic their cynicism. Tiny-hearted is as tiny-hearted does.

The only kind of people I should be giving my time of day are the *Inner home souls* searching for *their pack* to run their Dreams clear into **REAL**ity with.

To all those *courageous once beaten down souls,* the ones Michael Meade speaks of in the following quote,

The fateful event of being wounded early in life creates the need for a deep healing process that becomes (the) path of the awakening for each person...

Life sees you! Life salutes you! Life loves you! You Go Girl! You Go Boy!

POEM: Why?

I had a dream last night
that I died and The Lord
asked me, why?
Why, when I was alive, I
wasn't myself?
And all the excuses that had once
served me well, now didn't mean a thing,
because in Truth? I never dared
go out on **That** Limb,
To the place the Lord later shared, held
Her Most Precious Fruits -
A Place where I never could lose.

I cried that night, deep, bitter tears of regret,
then tears of Joy when I arose, and realised
there was still time, yet.

And never again did I forget
to **RE**-member myself –
and **RE-spond to The Call** to share and
express,
those God, Given, Talents.

Epilogue: On Being Human, Kind

I Am Because We Are.
- Ubuntu African Proverb

POEM: Satisfaction Guaranteed

So satisfying living a life
fully grounded in me -
not according to how
others think I should be.

Riding out the storms,
flowing with the natural rhythms of life,
no longer hiding behind
difficulties and strife.

Self-abnegation?
A thing of the past,
free to just Be - at last!

Going for it all
my heart's desire,
passions alive, and on fire.

Satisfying my Soul,
reaching my goal -
on course;
a destiny unfolds.

Deep and dark
the essence of me
loving myself,
unconditionally.

Beautiful and Broad,
Powerful and Free,
Extraordinary woman -
That's me!

On The Rat Race:
Tick Tock

Tick Tock, Tick Tock, Tick Tock

She wakes late, nothing new
once again promising to
get to bed early tonight.

Then in the bathroom, she looks into
the mirror of more lies and tell herself,
"Definitely, today, I will treat myself right".

Breakfast time arrives, and she starts to take real
  good care of herself, by
denying her body the fuel it needs to get its head
  around
behind the steering wheel of her life.

Then she rationalises,

"I feel just fine, I'm just not an eat first thing in the
    morning kind of child".

She arrives subconsciously, deliberately late
to a job working for and with people she secretly
    despises and claims to hate,
but which nevertheless pays - not the forever
    never-ending cycles of bills -
and robs her of the Will to question and reason,
"Who am I? Why am I here?"

She continues to love herself so much she decides
    to skip lunch -
although she back door slide draw in two chunky
    chocolate bars
for an instant high; that should keep her still.

At four thirty she wonders why the last hour
    always slithers by
so desperate she is to leave behind this workplace
    where she
waste so much of her time.

Now she's counting down the stations to destina-
    tion 'home life',
after wasting even more time playing, 'avoiding
    passengers eyes
whilst hiding behind same old titillating news
    headlines'.

She arrives home late - seven thirty, a quarter to
    eight,
after being repossessed by, "I've been so good to
    myself today -
haven't eaten a thing all day" Chinese takeaway -
as well as two more chocolate bars, two big packet
    of crisps,
some cigs for a spliff, and a bottle of rosé to go
    with it.

She washes and night-dresses, beginning to
    prepare herself for her
9 o'clock never-ending date of comfort food eating
    herself.
She eats, drinks, smokes 'til she's physically
    overspent,
though deep down her spirit still feels ever so
    under nourished.

Feeling empty and alone, she reaches out, makes
    contact, telephone,
calling a friend and in misery like-minded
    company together
bemoan their life condition- though they dress it
    up in
other people's -isms and -kisms.

Then in the early hours of the morn,
she falls asleep on sofa, exhausted, forlorn,

as her Soul resumes complete control, and sighs,
Maybe tomorrow she'll arise and quit
this God forsaken Rat-Race-Going- Nowhere,
    Fast-Times.

"Then again, better not leave it purely to chance -
that wouldn't be wise, I will make a visit in her
    dreams
as he sleeps tonight. I know exactly which dream I
    will grace them
with my Presence, the One where they Arise, and
    Realise
that the real nightmare is the story of their unlived
waking lives."

On Inhumanity:
The Problem Of The Human Heart

In real time, whilst writing and putting this project, my second book, together for publication, I was so incredibly incensed yesterday (March 17th 2022) by the story and report of a 15-year-old school girl in Hackney London England who was sexually abused and totally humiliated by two female police officers, and a school very much implicit in the crime. This crime against humanity was committed in 2020 during the heat of the trauma that was Covid-19 and the racist murder - one amongst very many - of George Floyd.

I was ranting about it to my therapist - I allow myself to **RE**-turn to therapy as and when needed as I continue to grow and become the all that I may be - and we concluded that having made that decision to strip search a 15 year old girl, called by the media Child Q, without her parents being presented, least of all be informed of the matter; that being objectified and humiliated in this inhumane way, the officers had to have already reduced her to a *NO THING* in their minds. **Adultification** of children and reducing them to no things in the heart and the mind, is a tenet of racism; an Adultification very similar to paedophiles malignant thought patterns around their justifications of their molestation of children.

As I was talking to my therapist - who is a white woman, one who is wise and woke - I realised more deeply that, people who treat other fellow human beings like this, especially *a child,* act from a corrupt, inhuman, frozen over heart and soul. Loving caring humane human beings cannot behave like this... So, who is the animal?

My therapist reminded me that, even animals feel. Apologies animals. Perhaps I should call these kinds of humans, uncivilised. *Unhumanised.*

My therapist also said words to the effect of, this inhumanity that such people can dish out so easily, without second thought, is what Desmond Tutu spoke at lengths about in his Call, especially about the Apartheid that was, and still is, being worked out in South Africa. There was no "...and they all lived happily ever after" when Apartheid was finally declared the inhumane system that it was, just like there was no happy ever after when Slavery was so-called 'abolished'.

This Child Q subject and situation was all very triggering for me being a survivor of childhood sexual abuse; being black and a woman; being a mother, an aunt, etc... *being human.*

So, I just had to write this Matter of Heart *Out...*

Oswald J. Smith once said,

The heart of the human problem, is the problem of the human heart.

I believe this to be true.

Some folks are in serious need of heart transplants, also known as *Self-Transformation.* Some much more than others. And when it comes to trauma that is metered out in society at the hands of law enforcement, by powers that be, who are supposed to be there to protect and serve us, trauma recovery must come from both the personal and the collective systemic side of things. As the following statement from Dr Maria Peredes **RE**-Minds...

While trauma informed therapy is important, social justice informed therapy is even more important. One cannot fully practice trauma informed therapy without understanding the trauma of social injustice...

And still, we rise...

On Therapy:
Personal Political

Oftentimes, our source of inner conflict and dis-ease are linked with the sources of conflict in society. These inner conflicts arise from deeply entrenched value judgements that stem from certain groups of people holding the power to determine the lives of others. It is for this reason that *therapy can be likened to political activity.*

As well as being used to uphold and enforce traditional value judgements, therapy can hold potent the opportunity to challenge some of our society's current values, especially in the area of *valuing different people.* Therapy - and services and loving relationships like it - at its best, offers us an opportunity to **RE**-evaluate ourselves and our lives within a ***Framework of Equality***... If we choose - and dare - to allow therapy to take us to those depths.

The work that is undertaken in therapy consists of struggling to understand the conflicting forces operating inside us, as well as questioning and challenging the forces operating in the world outside.

This form of therapy has true love for humanity at its core, as it strives continually towards deeply valuing *all* human beings, regardless of their behaviour. In therapy, one of the main drives is to *understand the reasons behind problematic and unkind behaviours, towards self and others.*

On the topic of this love for humanity type of therapy, in her book, 'Understanding Ourselves, The Uses of Therapy', Joan Woodward says,

This ideology is viewed as subversive/threatening to the establishment, because it so strongly challenges the currently held ideologies based on seeking power, the idealising of war and the savouring of the spoils of exploitation. These are largely male ideologies, which have dominated the world and now threatens its very existence.

I would add that these ideologies are largely *white male* ideologies.

I very much work in this individual and society **RE**-evaluative way. Not all therapists do.

When we do work in this way, we come into the arena of political; of Activism. Hard times call for real measures. Real shifters and shakers are out there, in and at all stations where real lasting difference is there to be made. So, if you are thinking about therapy for yourself, take your time and shop/look around for the right therapist for you. When it comes to therapy, there are now more richer pickings than there have ever been, especially this side of the shores Post George Floyd and the trauma that was Covid-19.

And I repeat, again here,

While trauma informed therapy is important, social justice informed therapy is even more important. One cannot fully practice trauma informed therapy without understanding the trauma of social injustice...

It *IS* time for change.

We can't be sitting on the fence like the old days. Go heal your heart if it is hardened and walled off. We are made for greater things than this! We have become so terribly distracted. We need to change the malignant form we find ourselves living with and in. We are to heal and unburden the heart, and come again in a more Humane Life Form.

It is time to Humane-Up!

Rise Up and Wise Up!

It's Now o' Clock!!

POEM: Eye Have A Dream

Eye have a Dream..
Eye see You, Eye see We
I see Eye have a Dream.
Eye See One Big Happy Family,
Unified In More Human(e)ised Communities,
Creating Untold Opportunities...

And in this Dream, We are **all the more**
Real In True Identity,
And Our natures -
though varying in degrees -
Is always – *All Ways*-
of Universal Pedigree.

In this Dream that Eye does See,
We Are Good - God – All - Mighty

Free -
At Last!
For It all starts with a Genesis Dream -
as what the I can't See
The Mind's Eye can't bring to True Love
to Conceive.

So, let's set our own Sights Free,
Tap and *Lean **IN**-to*
Like-Hearted Energy,
for that, in itself, will guarantee the humane in you
of A More Joyous and Just society,
Coming Forth Day By Day
In True Identity.

And to the Earth Plane -
at the very least you'll leave -
A Love Legacy that nourishes and feeds
The Eye In Us
That *Needs* to Dream...

And Truly Live,
and Be,
As
Originally Intended.

There is no mistakes made In Creation.

Nature Loves Originals!
And has created All Her Life Forms
To Be...
One Of A (Humane) Kind.

The Time Is Now,
To Live as Originally Intended;
To Turn
Back Around on This Mission
That Is
Far From Impossible - if you/we ***truly*** want it.

Amongst other things -
I Am -
Denise Marcia James:

The Dream and The Hope
Of The Slave,
In This Time,
RE*-Turned.*

Peace, Love and Light, All Ways, ***Always.***

October 2022

About The Author

Denise is a 57-year-old Mother of 2 sons and an overjoyed Grandmother of 5.

She works as a Psychotherapist in a thriving Private Practice. She has a huge belief in the transformative power of creativity and learning and growing through the sharing of experiences.

She is a lover of life who is passionate about mental health and well-being and raising awareness around those subjects, as well as the negative impact of Adverse Childhood experiences. She abhors injustice in all its forms and does not shy away from questioning and challenging injustice in her day-to-day life and on her platforms.

Denise became a first-time published author - a dream come true and through - on 7 th January 2021, when her book, **'Back To Love',** was released.

About that book, Denise says...

'Back To Love' shares and tells the story of my self-rediscovery, as well as psychological, spiritual, social, and racial healing Journey, undertaken after experiencing, what was in 1987 called, a *Nervous Breakdown*. This Mental Health Crisis - which I go on to more aptly reframe as a *Spiritual Break-through* - was brought on by a range of traumas experienced in childhood and triggered at that time (1987) by the end of a difficult relationship, and struggles with a troubled relationship with food, namely Bulimia. This book offers hope and the message that, however one's life starts out, however the world tries to bury one in statistic, that there is *THAT SOMETHING inside sooo strong* that can help us make it through, begin again, and go on to live mostly joyous, purposeful, wholehearted lives.

Denise enjoys making dreams comes through. She loves music - especially what she calls "message music". She enjoys singing and dancing (her first loves), writing, reading, learning, good conversation, being in relationship, and overall living and loving well. She also enjoys keeping fit physically, emotionally, mentally, and spiritually.

References

1. Williams, Chancellor, (1992), Destruction of Black Civilisation: Great Issues of a Race from 4500BC to 2000AD, Third World Press, U.S.

2. Woodson, Carter Godwin, (1999), The Mis-Education of the Negro, 12th Media Services

3. Macy, Joanna, (2021) World as Lover, World as Self: Courage for Global Justice and Planetary Renewal: Courage for Global Justice and Ecological Renewal, Parallax Press

4. Welsing, Dr. Frances Cress, (1974), Cress Theory of color-confrontation and Racism, The Black Scholar Journal of Black Studies and Research, Volume 5, 1974-issue 8: Black Health

5. Welsing, Frances C, (2004) The Isis Papers: The Keys to the Colors, African World Books

6. Fisher, Antwone Quenton, (2003), Finding Fish: A Memoir, Serpent's Tail

7. Antwone Fisher, (2003) Starring Derek Luke & Denzel Washington, Directed by Denzel Washington

8. The World Health Organisation, (2010, updated August 2014)

9. HEA, (1998) National Service Frameworks for Mental Health

10. IRIS, (2007-2010), Queen Mary University of London

11. Kaiser, Permanente, (1995-1997; Retrieved 25 March 2014), The Adverse Childhood Experience Study, Health Maintenance Organisation & Centre for Disease, Control & Prevention

12. Mental Health Foundation, Registered Charity No. England 801130

13. Mental Health Cost to the Economy (updated 2010) Centre for Mental Health Policy Paper 2003

14. Mental Health Act, (1983, 2007), Mental Health Capacity Act, 2005

15. Kolk, Van der, B.A., & Fisher, R (1995, in press), Dissociation & The Fragmentary Nature of Traumatic Memories: Background & Experimental Evidence. Journal of Traumatic Stress.

16.Solace Women's Aid, Rape Crisis, Non-profit organisation, London, England

17.James, Denise, (2021), Back to love, That Guy's House, now known as, The Good House.

18.The BBC1, (Monday 23rd October 2006), Series 3 Episode 3 of 8, Who Do You Think You Are, Colin Jackson

19.A Ministry of Justice publication under section 95 of the Criminal Justice Act 1991, Statistics on Race and the Criminal Justice System (2018), Published 28 November 2019

20.Goleman, Daniel, (1996), Emotional Intelligence: Why it Can Matter More Than IQ, Bloomsbury Publishing PLC

21.Caruso, David R, (2004), The Emotional Intelligent Manager: How to Develop and Use the Four Key Emotional Skills of Leadership, John Wiley & Sons Inc

22. Salovey, P, Ph.D. Brackett, Marc A. & Mayer, John, (2004), Emotional Intelligence: Key Readings on the Mayer and Salovey Model, Natl Professional Resources Inc

23. Supertramp, (1979), Breakfast in America, The Logical Song, 1979 Company Sleeve, Vinyl

24. Bradshaw, John, (1991), Home Coming: Reclaiming and Championing Your Inner Child, Little, Brown Book

Group

25. Montagu, Ashley, (1988) Growing young second edition, Praeger

26. Gottman, John, (1998), Raising An Emotionally Intelligent Child, Prentice Hall & IBD

27. Wilde, Stuart, (1996), Infinite Self: 33 Steps to Reclaiming Your Inner Power, Hay House

28. Wilde, Stuart & Krepcik, Chris, (2012) The Fringe Dwellers Guide To Almost Everything, Tolemac

29. O'Malley, Mary, (2004), The Gifts of Our Compulsions: A Revolutionary Approach to Self-Acceptance and Healing, New World Library

30. Lesser, Elizabeth, (2017), Marrow: Love, Loss, and What Matters Most, HarperWave

31. Roosevelt, Theodore, (1910) The Man in the Arena, Theodore Roosevelt Center at Dickson State University. Retrieved 2019-05-24

32. Brown, Brene, (2015), Daring Greatly: How the Courage to Be Vulnerable Transforms the Way We Live, Love, Parent, and Lead, Penguin Life

33. Lerner, Harriet (2004) The Dance of Anger: A Woman's Guide to Changing the Patterns of Intimate Relationships, Element books

34. Hooks, Bell (2014) ain't I a woman, Routledge; 2nd edition,

35. Hooks, Bell (2014) Sisters of the yam, black women and self-Recovery, Routledge; 2nd edition

36. Walker, Alice (2005) In Search of Our Mothers' Gardens, W&N

37. Local Child Safeguarding Practice Review-Child Q, (March 2022),

38. Tutu, Desmond M, (2015), The Book of Forgiving: The Fourfold Path for Healing Ourselves and Our World, Harper Collins Paperbacks

39. Welwood, John (2007) Perfect Love, Imperfect Relationships, Shambhala Publications Inc

40. Mathabane, Mark & Jackson, J.D Narrator (2018) The Lessons of Ubuntu: How African Philosophy Can Inspire Healing in America, Brilliance Audio; Unabridged edition

41. Diop, Cheikh Anta, (1988) Precolonial Black Africa: A Comparative Study of the Political and Social Systems of Europe and Black Africa, from Antiquity to the Formation of Modern States , Lawrence Hill Books

42.Woodward, Joan, (1988), Understanding Ourselves: Uses of Therapy, Palgrave Macmillan

43. Meade, Michael, (2018) Awakening the Soul: A Deep Response to a Troubled World, Greenfirepr

Printed in Great Britain
by Amazon